GEMS OF THEORIES

JALSON JACOB & SARAN S.

Contents

Contents

Foreword

Dr. Arun George
Assistant Professor
Department of English
Government College Kottayam

Students of literature should be encouraged to ask theoretical questions about the novels, stories and poems they come across so that they could find new layers of meaning in these works of art. In short, familiarizing them with the different literary theories give them a toolbox for approaching any literary text. I am happy that this collection of essays mainly based on literary theories, will provide the readers with a new perspective of understanding theories. Each chapter aims to give an in-depth analysis of the different literary theories. I wish all readers a delightful and enriching learning experience.

Editor

Dr. Jalson Jacob
Associate Professor
Department of English
Government College Kottayam

Dr. Jalson Jacob is an Associate Professor of English at Government College Kottayam. He has completed his Doctoral Degree in ELT from the University of Kerala in 2020. His areas of interest include teacher training and material production. He is the author of several articles published in various national and international journals.

Editor

Saran S.
Assistant Professor & Head
Department of English
University Institute of Technology-Pathiyoor
University of Kerala

Saran S. (MA, Ph. D.) is a writer, Poet, Nature Activist, Teacher, and Research Scholar. He has completed his Doctoral Research from the Department of English, M. S. University in 2020. Currently, he is working as an Assistant Professor and Head in the Department of English, University Institute of Technology Pathiyoor, University of Kerala. His areas are Comparative Literature, Cultural Studies, Film Studies, Psychoanalytical Studies and Eco

Studies. He is the author of several articles published in various national and international journals as well as six academic books on topics of current interest like English Language, Film Studies, Partition Studies and Cultural Studies. He also authored a collection of poems and short stories. He also edited twenty-two international books. He is the chief editor of Edit Academic, an advisory board member and Associate Editor in *The Creative Launcher*, international, open access, peer-reviewed refereed, e-journal in English and also Editorial Board Member in *Shodhkosh: Journal of Visual and Performing Arts* (UGC-Care Listed Journal).

Contributors

1. "Analysis on Role of Society in Identity Crisis of Transgenders"**Dr. Roselin Linitta George**, Assistant Professor, Sanpada College of Commerce and Technology, Sanpada West, Navi Mumbai, Maharashtra.
2. "Partition of India: Problematizing the Rehabilitation of Abducted Women" - **Shahana Mukherjee & Dr. Antara Ghatak.**
3. "The Survivor of Heyday: Flavour of Ecofeminism in the *Handmaid's Tale*" - **Joshna Francis**, Assistant Professor on Contract, Bhavan's College of Arts & Commerce, Kakkanad, Ernakulam.
4. "Willing Suspension of Disbelief: A Mythical Journey through Njan Gandharvan and Tumbhad" - **Neethu Anna Tharakan**, Assistant Professor, Department of English, Mar Ivanios College, Trivandrum.
5. "Psychotic Disorders Lead to Savagery" - **Ms. Charanprit Kaur**, Asst.Teacher, St. Anthony's High School, Mumbai.
6. "Narrating Female Bildung" - **Ms. Lalitha Sarma R.**, Doctoral Research Scholar, Dept. of English, Sri Sathya Sai Institute of Higher Learning, Anantapur Campus.
7. "The New Generation Natwarlal's of Cyberspace" - **Asha P. Alias, a**ssistant Professor, Department Of Computer Science, Yeldo Mar Baselios College, Kothamangalam.
8. "Taking a Second Look at the Lenses: Deconstructing Fantasised Womanhood in Malayalam Cinema" – **Treesa Petreena**, Ph. D. Research Scholar, St. Xavier's College for Women, Aluva

Introduction

Gems of Theories

The corpus of concepts and methods we utilise in the practical study of literature is referred to as "literary theory." We don't mean the meaning of a piece of literature when we say literary theory; we mean the theories that indicate what literature might signify. Literary theory is an explanation of the fundamental ideas, or tools, that we use to try to understand literature. All literary interpretation has a theoretical foundation, yet it can be used to justify a wide range of critical activities. Literary theory examines the significance of race, class, and gender for literary research, both from the position of the author's biography and an analysis of their thematic content.

Literary theory," sometimes designated "critical theory," or "theory," and now undergoing a transformation into "cultural theory" within the discipline of literary studies, can be understood as the set of concepts and intellectual assumptions on which rests the work of explaining or interpreting literary texts. Literary theory refers to any principles derived from internal analysis of literary texts or from knowledge external to the text that can be applied in multiple interpretive situations. All critical practice regarding literature depends on an underlying structure of ideas in at least two ways: theory provides a rationale for what constitutes the subject matter of criticism—"the literary"—and the specific aims of critical practice—the act of interpretation itself.

Within the discipline of literary studies, literary theory, also known as "critical theory" or "theory," and now undergoing a transformation into "cultural theory," can be defined as the set of concepts and intellectual assumptions upon which the work of explaining or interpreting literary texts is based. Any ideas produced from internal analysis of literary texts or from knowledge outside the text that can be applied in numerous interpretive scenarios are referred to as literary theory. In at least two ways, all critical practises in the field of literature is based on an underlying structure of ideas: theory gives an explanation for what constitutes the subject matter of criticism—"the literary"—and the specific goals of critical practice—the process of interpretation itself.

Literary theory and formal practise of literary interpretation follow a similar but less well-known path to the history of philosophy, and can be found in the historical record dating back to Plato. Plato's meditation on the relationship between words and the things to which they refer can be found in the Cratylus. Plato's scepticism regarding signification, i.e., that words have no etymological relationship to their meanings and are "imposed" randomly, becomes a fundamental concern to both "Structuralism" and "Post-structuralism" in the twentieth century. Throughout most of Western history, however, a consistent conviction in "reference," or the idea that words and images correspond to an objective reality, has provided epistemological (that is, knowledge-related) support for theories of literary representation.

During the nineteenth century, modern literary theory progressively arises in Europe. German "higher criticism" subjected biblical texts to severe historicizing that broke with orthodox scriptural interpretation in one of the earliest breakthroughs of literary theory. "Higher," or "source criticism," looked at biblical stories in light of similar stories from other cultures, a strategy that foreshadowed parts of the method and spirit of twentieth-century thought, particularly "Structuralism" and "New Historicism." In France, eminent literary critic Charles Augustin Saint Beuve claimed that a work of literature could be completely explained in terms of biography, while novelist Marcel Proust devoted his life to refuting Saint Beuve in a massive narrative in which he claimed that the details of the artist's life are utterly transformed.

Attention to the etymology of the term "theory," from the Greek "theoria," alerts us to the partial nature of theoretical approaches to literature. "Theoria" indicates a view or perspective of the Greek stage. This is precisely what literary theory offers, though specific theories often claim to present a complete system for understanding literature. The current state of theory is such that there are many overlapping areas of influence, and older schools of theory, though no longer enjoying their previous eminence, continue to exert an influence on the whole. The once widely-held conviction (an implicit theory) that literature is a repository of all that is meaningful and ennobling in the human experience, a view championed by the Leavis School in Britain, may no longer be acknowledged by name but remains an essential justification for the current structure of American universities and liberal arts curricula. The moment of "Deconstruction" may have passed, but its emphasis on the indeterminacy of signs (that we are unable to establish exclusively what a word means when used in a given situation) and thus of texts, remains significant. Many critics may not embrace the label "feminist," but the premise that gender is a social construct, one of theoretical feminisms distinguishing insights, is now axiomatic in a number of theoretical perspectives.

While literary theory has always implied or directly expressed a conception of the world outside the text, in the twentieth century three movements—"Marxist theory" of the Frankfurt School, "Feminism," and "Postmodernism"—have opened the field of literary studies into a broader area of inquiry. Marxist approaches to literature require an understanding of the primary economic and social bases of culture since Marxist aesthetic theory sees the work of art as a product, directly or indirectly, of the base structure of society. Feminist thought and practice analyses the production of literature and literary representation within the framework that includes all social and cultural formations as they pertain to the role of women in history. Postmodern thought consists of both aesthetic and epistemological strands.

Postmodernism in art has included a move toward non-referential, non-linear, abstract forms; a heightened degree of self-preferentiality; and the collapse of categories and conventions that had traditionally governed art. Postmodern thought has led to the serious questioning of the so-called metanarratives of history, science, philosophy, and economic and sexual reproduction. Under postmodernity, all knowledge comes to be seen as "constructed" within historical self-contained systems of understanding. Marxist, feminist, and postmodern thought have brought about the incorporation of all human discourses (that is, interlocking fields of language and knowledge) as a subject matter for analysis by the literary theorist. Using the various poststructuralist and postmodern theories that often draw on disciplines other than the literary—linguistic, anthropological, psychoanalytic, and philosophical—for their primary insights, literary theory has become an interdisciplinary body of cultural theory. Taking as its premise that human societies and knowledge consist of texts in one form or another, cultural theory (for better or worse) is now applied to the varieties of texts, ambitiously undertaking to become the preeminent model of inquiry into the human condition.

Literary theory is a site of theories: some theories, like "Queer Theory," are "in;" other literary theories, like "Deconstruction," are "out" but continue to exert an influence on the field. "Traditional literary criticism," "New Criticism" and "Structuralism" are alike in that they held to the view that the study of literature has an objective body of knowledge under its scrutiny. The other schools of literary theory, to varying degrees, embrace a postmodern view of language and reality that calls into serious question the objective referent of literary studies. The following categories are certainly not exhaustive, nor are they mutually exclusive, but they represent the major trends in literary theory of this century.

CHAPTER I

ANALYSIS ON ROLE OF SOCIETY IN IDENTITY CRISIS OF TRANSGENDERS

Dr. Roselin Linitta George

Assistant Professor

Sanpada College of Commerce and Technology

Sanpada West, Navi Mumbai, Maharashtra.

Abstract

Gender is the word that is defined as one's identity as female or male or as entirely male. Where Trans is defined as a person whose sense of personal identity and gender does not correspond with their sex. In that sense, Transgender, a biological and social minority or as a belief, indicate the identity crisis and contrast of practices that demonstrated between or beyond the classification of male or female. Transgender people have a gender identity or gender expression that differs from their sex assigned at birth. The trans community is incredibly diverse. Social attitudes to transgender persons and other gender minorities vary around the world, and in many traditions, preconception and social stigma are common. Society even in this 21st century still not understood who is trans? What is trans? What are types of trans? Society is still in a stereotype belief that there are only two kinds of categories Men and Women. Our society has a set of ideas about gender. This results in a tension of identity crisis that adversely affects the physical and mental status of trans people that categorized as (LGBTQIA) straight, bisexual, lesbian, gay, asexual, pansexual, queer etc. This paper discusses and analyzes the social attitude towards transgenders and the identity crisis they face during a lifetime.

Keywords: Gender, Trans and LGBTQIA community.

• • •

Analysis on Role of Society in Identity Crisis of Transgenders

Gender identity is the personal sense of one's own gender. Culture determines gender roles and what is masculine and feminine. Gender identity is defined as a personal conception of oneself as male or female (or rarely, both or neither). An identity crisis is a developmental event that involves a person questioning their sense of self or place in the world. This concept is intimately related to the concept of gender role, which is defined as the outward manifestations of personality that reflect gender identity. We're born our gender identity is no secret. We're either a boy or a girl. From here we should start thinking about the other side of gender identity. Other than a firm belief of being men or women there's a group of people around as who born different.

Transgender people have a gender identity or gender expression that differs from the sex that they were assigned at birth. If one's gender identity matches the gender assigned at birth, this is called cis-gender. But, if a sense of unease or dissatisfaction that a person may have because of a contradiction between their biological sex and their gender identity.

Jack Drescher, a New York psychiatrist who was a part of the American Psychiatric Association's workgroup on gender identity, revised the latest manual on mental disorders, the (Diagnostic and Statistical Manual Disorders) DSM-5. He says, usually, with a mental disorder, we try and change the person's mind. "This is the only mental disorder where the treatment is changing the body. In a typical mental disorder, we try to make those symptoms go away. Drescher says, 'It's not called a disorder, but it is in the handbook of mental disorders.

Gender Dysphoria

Gender identity typically develops in stages: Childhood, Teenage, Youth. Children experience serious distress that results from an incongruence between one's sex assigned at birth and one's gender identity it is called "Gender Dysphoria". A child's gender identity isn't always indicative of one particular gender expression, the expression and behaviours might be bathroom behaviour, selection of toys, selection of dress etc. Make sure the family gives time to the child to tell what they feel.

Unfortunately, transgender teens receive near-constant reminders that their body and mind are not in sync, when they are not allowed to transition, they may suffer from depression, anxiety and an increased risk of inflicting self-harm. Although a possibility of discrimination occurs in school also. Sexual minority status is a key risk factor for suicide among lesbian, gay, bisexual youth; however, it has not been studied among transgender youth. Transgender youth are usually dependent on their parents for care, shelter, financial support, and other needs transgender youth face different challenges compared to adults.

Unfortunately, transgender youth still experience high levels of harassment, bullying, discrimination and even family rejection. When parents and families of transgender youth talk openly about those concerns, it can provide support to those who are still struggling with their own fears. The phenomenon of people who identify as another gender is a relatively new concept in the scientific world and an even newer concept to society. The word 'transgender' did not appear until the publication of Harry Benjamin's seminal publication, The Transsexual Phenomenon. In his 1966 work, Benjamin creates three categories; those who "merely want to 'dress', go out 'dressed', and to be accepted as women," those who find themselves in a "more severe stage of an emotional disturbance," and those who are fully transexual. In describing transsexuality, Benjamin notes the alienation from society that transgendered people experience. The transgender community has been listed as a criminal tribe since a century ago during the British empire and since then has been misunderstood, ostracized, marginalized and discriminated against till today.

The ignorance has driven out many transgenders from home and families and till today, many transgenders have remained beggars seeking rights and have been exploited sexually. Though trans considered the worst people a huge number of socially respected people utilize them sexually because they are now even an oppressed community. Why did all Trans people consider sex workers by society? Is that true? Why are trans people not getting educated? Why trans not doing job in medical fields, IT area, or in any corporate companies explains? What explains public opinion towards transgender people, rights, and candidates? Through this chapter, we discuss and explains attitudes regarding (1) the personal characteristics of transgender people ;(2) a variety of transgender rights; and (3) transgender candidates for public office. Lack of knowledge in Law, Transgenders are being badly attacked by society. The Transgender Persons (Protection of Rights)

Act, 2019 ('Transgender Persons Act') seeks to recognize the identity of transgender persons and prohibit discrimination in, inter alia, the fields of education, employment, healthcare, holding or disposing of property, holding public or private office and access to and Society has failed to accept transgenders' gender identity due to which they have suffered from discrimination, social oppression and physical violence. Compared to other countries Trans people face challenges in India, the main problems that are being faced by the transgender community area of discrimination from employment, educational facilities, habitat, lack of medical facilities: like HIV and hygiene, depression, hormone pill abuse, tobacco and alcohol abuse, and problems related to marriage and adoption.

Misinterpretation about the term 'transgender'

Transgender is not an expression restricted to persons whose pudenda are intermixed but it is a cover term of people whose gender expression, identity or behaviour differs from the norms expected from their birth sex. Various transgender identities fall under this category including transgender male, (MTF) and female to male (FTM). It also includes cross-dressers (Those who wear clothes of the other), genderqueer people (they feel they belonged to either both genders or neither gender) and transsexuals.

Abuse affects the Transgender Community

One of the most fundamental principles of being in a relationship is to love and accept someone for who they are. Now, we don't mean accepting unhealthy tendencies, like a quick temper and being overly critical, but more the unique things that make someone special. Woefully, our society not usually shows acceptancy and kindness towards the things that make someone special, especially when it comes to people who don't obey conventional gender identities. Sometimes it's prime to show love to someone specifically anyone who identifies as transgender, is to love them for the betterment of their life and it's vital. We at one cherish and accept that everybody merits a sound relationship and know that each individual took a place in our development for later. And whereas the subtleties of a relationship can contrast depending on how you identify marginalized communities may confront particular challenges. Here we discuss the several cases of abuse from a society that affects the identity reveal of the transgender community:

(1) Relationship abuse

(2) They confront separation and battle to be accepted

(3) Their identity and sexuality can be utilized against them

(4) Solid relationship models are hard to find for Trans

(5) Obscured gender identity may make it harder to recognize mishandle

(6) Limited resources to help Trans people

(8) Higher Suicide Rate

Domestic abuse also called "domestic violence "or "intimate partner violence", can be defined as a pattern of behaviour in any relationship but to trans people, the risk factor is high.30%-50% of trans communities experience dating violence compared to 20%-33% of the general population. Transgenders who face rejection from family and loved ones after revealing their identity are put through badgering and oppression. Trans people may face an identity crisis in personal life mainly because partners may try to abuse them using their identity by shaming them, making them feel inferior or making them feel they are born to be abused. Insulting verbally, by making a thought imposed on their mind that they are not good for anything, or they'll not be accepted or loved by anyone and all these thoughts leads to strong insecurity feel for trans people. Society shows high interest in playing on trans insecurity and sexual abuse as they don't have a strong partner Lack of healthy relationship of trans people with society leads to all physical and mental harassment. Often the legal system is against them, police and authorities show less interest in helping transgenders if they may abuse or harassed by the public or shows more eagerness to be convicted. Government authorities refuse to give valid documents for homeless transgenders for receiving government benefits as a citizen. All these practices should be changed because in this 21st century globalized world human and rational change is inevitable

How Society can support Transgenders?

- Educate ourselves about transgender issues. Allow trans-related in our book collection, make kids read from childhood, attend conferences etc.
- Make a good behavioural attitude towards people with a gender identity crisis.
- Support the right for trans people membership in various sociocultural identity groups (race, social class, disability, age, religion etc.)
- Avoid unwanted classification to maintain gender discrimination, and allow their names to be put as their identity.
- Make no conclusions about the sexual orientation of transgender people.
- Gender nonconformity is not synonymous with transgender identity. Not everyone who appears androgynous or who identifies as transgender or wants

gender affirmation treatment is transgender.
- Cleanse your mind to welcome transgenders in your friend circle, and help them.
- Ensure all legal support for trans people around us. Educate people around us about the rights of the trans community from our knowledge.
- Familiarize ourselves with provincial laws, local and state laws that protect trans people from harassment and discrimination.

The major findings and discussions of the study focused on the attempts made by the transgender for improving their image in society by requesting government jobs so that they contribute to social services. So, the government should think seriously about the welfare of trans people in any aspect. Let society never be a reason for the destruction for transgenders, and for making identity crisis, whereas society should stand for the uplifting trans community.

Works Cited

Elizabeth plumtree." How Gender Dysphoria Is Diagnosed,29,2021

Shaharban.Dr, IDENTITY CRISIS AND SOCIAL EXCLUSION-A STUDY ON TRANSGENDERS,2019.

Mrinalini S, TRANSGENDER IN SOCIETY Challenges and Solutions,2019

Faces of Cedars-Sinai, Dr, Maurice Garcia, Transgender Surgeon,2019

Ajay Amitabh Suman@ *AjayAmitabhSumanSpeaks*, MAR 30,2021

CHAPTER II

PARTITION OF INDIA: PROBLEMATIZING THE REHABILITATION OF ABDUCTED WOMEN

Shahana Mukherjee & Dr. Antara Ghatak

ABSTRACT

During the 1947 Partition of India, women were subjected to various kinds of violence by numerous agents. Thousands of women, Hindu, Muslim and Sikh were sexually violated, abducted, killed, forced to convert, forcefully married off on either side of the border. In the wake of rampant abductions during the Partition, the government came up with several rescue missions. The Abducted Persons (Recovery and Restoration) Act of 1949 was enforced temporarily by both the governments of India and Pakistan, aimed to rescue abducted persons and to hand them over to their families where they lawfully belonged. A Central Recovery Operation was carried out by the government of India between 1948 and 1956 with a similar purpose. Though these acts and operations helped many women back to their families, they denied women the agency to determine their habitation, overlooked individual predicament and the intricacies of human relationships in a patriarchal society where a woman's body carries the burden of the honour of their communities. The question that then arises is- Were these women restored or further displaced? The present paper aims to examine the issue of abducted women and the gap that exists between the altruistic government policies to rescue, restore, and rehabilitate women and their hardships in reality- one which made them rethink questions of identity, home, and nation through the study of four short stories- *Embrace* and *The Stricken Daughter* by Ramapada Chowdhury, *Lajwanti* by Rajinder Singh Bedi, and *Exile* by Jamila Hashimi.

Keywords: abduction, identity, partition, rehabilitation, women.

Introduction

The partition of India in 1947 was both news of celebration of the independence of India as well as of horrors that accompanied it. The partition of the Indian subcontinent was an agonising tragedy for people on both sides of the border as it inflicted violence on human bodies and human lives. The communal riots triggered inconceivable acts of violence and women were the worst victims of this catastrophic moment in the history of India. They were raped, abducted, converted, forcefully married off, killed, paraded naked on streets, their genitalia mutilated and their bodies were tattooed with the emblem of the 'other' religious community. These ghastly acts of violence indicate that women were reduced to their bodies which became a site of a contest for the opposing religious communities and their bodies became hieroglyphs on which was inscribed the violent history of the division of India and Pakistan.

Of twelve million people who were estimated to be affected by the Partition, eighty thousand of them reportedly were women who were. It was in the wake of such rampant abductions that both the governments of India and Pakistan decided to set up rescue missions to restore such victims to where they 'rightfully belonged'.

Thus, between 1948 and 1956, The Central Recovery Operation and The Abducted Persons (Recovery and Restoration) Act was initiated to bring back the abducted citizens of the nation, reunite them with their families and reintegrate them as a part of society. The police along with women social workers like Mridula Sarabhai, Kamlabehn Patel helped recover many women from the other side of the border. These rescue missions may have yielded outstanding results but the recovery of abducted victims cannot be termed synonymous with their rehabilitation.

The newly formed Indian state which majorly was a Hindu nation and its preoccupation with the idea of their women embodying communal and national honour is predominantly what made the lives of war struck women complicated. Women often chose self-demolition to preserve their 'purity' when their men failed to protect them during communal riots. The abducted victims had a reluctant response on being recovered and often expressed a desire to stay back with their abductors in fear of not being accepted by their families and communities as their 'purity' had been 'polluted'. Some of them had borne children with their abductors and settled down with them. The government however assuming the role of a father patriarch, decided their fate. The newly formed Indian nation though claimed to be secular, determined the nationality of these women based on their religion; Hindu and Sikh women were assumed naturally to be Indians and Muslims as Pakistanis. The recovery and rehabilitation policy of the government was altruistic as though it claimed to reunite abducted women with their families, give them a free environment to live in and give them citizenship, they were patriarchal and driven by an incentive to avenge the loss of national honour. The recovery policies overlooked the myriad intricacies of human relationships and individual predicament, these women were denied political rights and agency to determine their residence and were exchanged like chattel without their consent. Therefore, the question that then arises is whether these women were successfully restored or further displaced.

Apart from facts and figures as recorded by the government and the testimony of the social workers associated with the recovery process, very little documentation can be found about the real experiences of these women. Their voices though have been silenced by trauma and patriarchal forces experiences have been given expression in works of literature that elaborate the manifold consequences that abducted women have had to face. The government failed to realize that rescuing and reuniting abducted women were not enough to rehabilitate them in a society where the honour of a community is vested in the bodies of womenfolk. Therefore, in the course of this paper, I intend to closely read four short stories-*Embrace*, *The Stricken Daughter*, *Lajwanti* and *Exile* that present the destiny of abducted women and trace the gap between formulated government plans to rehabilitate and restore these women and their experience of reuniting with their families and their restoration in society.

• • •

Historiographical Background and Theoretical Premise

The Partition of India in 1947, marked the end of a 200-year long colonial rule by the British imperialists as a result of the long-standing communal difference between the Hindus and the Muslims. The first attempt at partitioning the state of India can be traced back to 1905 when as the result of an uprising nationalist movement in Bengal, the colonial government created a Muslim majority province of East Bengal and Assam alongside Bengal. Bengal was however again reunified as a single province in 1911 due to the rising intensity of the nationalist movement which was slowly spreading to all parts of the nation. Demanding a separate representation and electorate for the Muslims, the All India Muslim League was founded in Bengal. Throughout the 1920s and 30s, the rift between the two communal parties continued. The colonial rulers found them in a compromising situation, the colonial rulers decided to comply with the demand of full self-governance of India. A new interim government was thus set up with the two political parties- Congress and All India Muslim but it, however, failed to operate peacefully amidst rising communal tension in the northern and eastern part of the state. Partition seemed to be the only solution to this long-standing issue and Lord Mountbatten's resolution of dividing the nation in June 1947 made sure that the new nation-states, India and Pakistan remained enemies for years to come.

The Partition of 1947 brought about large-scale migration, violence, death, sexual assault and prolonged trauma that followed as a result. The two new nations that emerged based on religion, gave rise to communal scission. Women were not only witnesses to this violence but also became objects of violence. Within patriarchal societies, women often have to bear the burden of embodying the honour of their community and they often were represented as the incarnation of the nation, especially by the Hindu nationalists during the Partition movement. Therefore, during a time of such ethnoreligious conflict, women became easy targets as an assault on them would signify defiling and emasculating the community she belonged to. During the communal riots, the bodies of women became contested sites upon which different communities strived hard to script their aspirations and authorities. They were reduced to the currency that determined the honour of their religious communities and the female body thus became cryptographs to partition violence; rape, sexual assault, abduction was inflicted upon them not to disgrace them but to tarnish the honour of the community and nation they belonged to. Often abducted women were converted and impregnated to mark an act of victory in changing their identity and in turn impairing the honour of their community. Paradoxically protecting and preserving the respect of women of one community, led to the violation of women from the 'other' community.

The government decided to take action to rescue victims of this ethnic chauvinism and after a meeting in September 1947, in Lahore, the Prime Ministers of India and Pakistan decided to launch a programme for rescuing abducted women on both sides of the border with the help of women social workers and police. The Central Recovery Operation came into action on 6th December 1947, after signing an Inter-Dominion Treaty and continued till 1956 with the aim of recovering abducted women and restoring them to their families where they rightfully belonged. In 1949 the Abducted Persons Recovery and Restoration Act was brought to force after the Indo-Pak government reached an agreement in November 1948, with the motive of recovering abducted persons. The act defined an 'abducted person' as a "male child under the age of sixteen years old or a female of whatever age who is, or immediately before the first day of March 1947, was a Muslim and who, on or after that day and before the 1ˢᵗ day of January 1949, has become separated from his or her family and found to be living with or under the control of any other individual or family, and in the latter case includes a child born to any such female after the said date" (23).

The state entrusted social workers, mostly women along with the help of the national police officers with the task of rescuing any person they suspected to have been abducted. Their primary work was to rescue these women with the help of the police and persuade those victims who were reluctant in leaving behind their new homes. The religious identities of the victims primarily determined their nationalities in the rescue mission and any confusion over whether the victim is an abducted person or not would be decided by a tribunal. Camps were set up to accommodate abducted persons till they were united with their families. This mission on account of outstanding work got extended and continued till 1955 rescuing approximately 22,000 Muslim women and about 8000 Sikh and Hindu women some brought back by force while some escaped happily.

A Second Exile: A Study of *The Stricken Daughter* and *Lajwanti*

Rampant abductions during the Partition led both the governments of the newly formed state of India and Pakistan to assume the role of the father patriarch and introduce corrective measures aimed at the well-being of abducted victims, that would not only restore women to their original homes but at the same time help restore the honour of their communities and the nation at large. The presence of such gender roles can be traced back to antiquity and its propagation is evident in the epic poem of *Ramayana* where Lord Rama's wife Sita, is abducted by the demon Ravana. The mythological story of Sita being rescued by the "hero King" Rama confronting and defeating the evil Ravana, can be paralleled to the situation of both Arundhati and Lajwanti who are representatives of many such women kidnapped by men of other religious communities during the Partition.

Rajinder Singh Bedi's *Lajwanti* is the story of a recovered abducted woman who was left behind in Pakistan by Babu Sunder Lal, her husband who migrated during the Partition and settled in Mohalla Shakoor in India where he began working as the secretary of a committee- 'rehabilitation of hearts' supporting the rehabilitation of recovered abducted women. They carried out processions every morning urging people to rehabilitate the abducted women in their hearts as in a predominantly Hindu society, where the woman is a quintessential symbol of sanctity, people like Narain Bawa in the story, representative of the majority of the society, showed disinclination in accepting women who were now converted and considered 'defiled'. Addressing the current situation of the recovered women, Prime Minister Nehru and Mahatma Gandhi made public appeals in favour of reintegrating abducted victims into society. Gandhi remarked, "I hear that women have this objection that the Hindus and not willing to accept back the recovered women because they say that they have become impure...if any of those recovered women should come to me, then I will give them as much respect and honour as I accord to these young maidens" (Bhasin and Menon 7). Sunder Lal, who had suffered a similar personal loss, reflected on being an abusive husband and hoping his Lajo would come back too, dedicated himself to the cause and thought to himself, "If I got another chance, I would really rehabilitate her in my heart...A society which refuses to accept these helpless women is beyond rotten beyond redemption and deserves to be liquidated" (Bedi 17). He argued that even though Lord Rama rescued Sita, she was later abjected from his Ram Rajya for no fault of her own. His Lajo and other abducted women are like Sita, innocent victims of violence and it is wrong to question their virtue when it is the wickedness of those like Ravana.

When one-day Lajwanti comes back at the Wagah Border where women were exchanged on either side of the border due to the efforts and supervision of social workers led by Mridula Sarabhai, Sunder Lal, unlike many other men who were hesitating to reclaim their women, brought back Lajwanti with him after her long exile. Unhappy neighbours kept away from Sunder Lal's house and he continued to promote the cause of the Rehabilitation of Hearts Committee with the same devotion. Though Sundar Lal had accepted Lajo, he had accepted her minus her body. Lajo wanted to narrate her experience in Pakistan at the hands of the abductor, share her trauma and sufferings the only way she could express and perhaps eventually part with her 'sinful' past but her voice was silenced by the reluctance of Sunder Lal who never broached the subject. He had enshrined Lajo at the inner sanctum of his house and even addressed her as 'Devi', not realizing that it established a distance between the deity and the worshipper. Lajo, who had accepted her fate as the wife of an abusive husband, on the other hand, yearned to redeem her old relationship with her husband. She realizes through Sunder Lal's devotee-like treatment towards her that the Partition had created a divide between her body and her soul and she was fated to live for the rest of her life a disembodied existence.

Set in Bengal against the backdrop of the Bengal Partition, which even though did not fall under the scope of the Abducted Persons Act of the government, presents a vivid picture of the fortune of recovered women through Ramapada Chowdhury's short story *The Stricken Daughter*. Abiding by the new rule of the state, Arundhati is brought back to her original home but she soon realizes "it wasn't to the same happy abode of the earlier times" (Chaudhuri 324). From the time she returns, her mother is bombarded with questions about her whereabouts for the five years she is way away and her justification of her daughter being at her in-laws' bears an underlying shame, a shame that Arundhati had feared would prevent her from being accepted back in her family. The story reveals that she had cried and begged the police to not take her back- "please don't take me back, I am quite alright and happy here...Even if I did go back, would I be able to get everything again? Will my parents, my brothers, my sister welcome me back amidst them once again?" (Chaudhuri 325). These words echo the concerns of many like Arundhati who were rescued as recorded in Butalia's *The Other Side of Silence*-"Why should I return? ...What is left in me now of religion or chastity" (Butalia 148) Arundhati had not returned alone, she had returned with a child born out of violence whom her mother suggested they send to an orphanage which would make their lives a little easier as otherwise, it would be a constant reminder of Arundhati's 'fallen state'. Amidst the daily reminder of the last chapter of her life and trying to live an ordinary life, while looking for a job she chanced upon her Subimalda whom she loved earlier.

Their conversation once again made Arundhati conscious of her regretful past and Subimalda's words- "Is there anything more to hide one's face for?" (329) made her apprehensive of her uneasy past that she could easily reveal to her neighbours is known to him too. It is revealed later that Subimal was referring to his sister Madhuri, who had fallen victim to the Partition violence. It is through Subimal's character that the mindset of a typical Hindu patriarch is revealed who is deeply ashamed because of her sister whom he now considers a 'fallen woman' and thinks "it would be better if she were not there" (333). Women, who were signifiers of a community's honour and purity, when violated were disregarded as unchaste and her return was not regarded as a heroic deed. The same is echoed in *Lajwanti* were refusing to accept the recovered women some said, "couldn't they have killed themselves? Why didn't they take poison and preserve their virtue and their honour? Why didn't they jump into a well? They are cowards, they clung to life" (Bedi 16). It was rather ideal for her to sacrifice her life to preserve the honour that her body carries which has led women to accept self-demolition several times in history and even during the Partition. Arundhati, who was hoping her Subimalda's mind had not changed despite the changing times, hoping to rebuild her life realizes her position in the society and it dawns upon her that it is perhaps better to lose one to riots like her family had lost her father than to return to only defame the family. Faced with her truth through the situation of her old companion Madhuri, she returns to her abductor with her child.

Therefore, many women like Lajo and Arundhati though were recovered, could never be restored to their prelapsarian state and thereby to the place and position they occupied in the family. If abducting them in itself was a crime that needed to be checked, then recovering and returning them by force to their families was a form of double abduction that they were subjected to. We see that Lajwanti when comes back, she looks much better and healthy to the dismay of Sunder Lal. She had already settled in her new life with her abductor who like Sunder Lal did not abuse her. Arundhati too similarly had settled in well living like a family with her abductor and their child. Her abductor had formed an attachment with her and the child that he writes about in the letter. Her abductor here in a way turns out to be her rescuer whom she returns to. Madhuri too, is revealed in the story, was recovered but ultimately goes back to her abductor unable to find social acceptance. Lajo on the other hand perceives that a split had been caused between her body and soul further alienating her from her husband terminating any possibility for her to recover her identity. These women were thus forced into a 'second exile' sometimes literally while sometimes in the corners of their own homes.

Identity and Belongingness in *Embrace* and *Banished*

The Partition violence that was inflicted upon women, was major to humiliate the other community which they thought was done best by converting women or impregnating them with children as it would leave behind a permanent corporal blemish, a marker of victory against the rival group. Following the recovery missions agreed upon by both the governments of India and Pakistan, missing complaints of female members were looked into and they were located with the objective of reuniting them with their families. The rescue teams faced resistance from the victim themselves on being recovered since they believed their communities would not take them back as they had been 'polluted' and would be deserted eventually and also because some did not want to part with the children they had borne with their abductors. In the definition of the 'abducted person', the Act included children born to women "who before the 1st day of March 1949, had become separated from her family and is found to be living with or under the control of an individual or a family" (Menon and Bhasin 4).

The governments agreed on nullifying any forced marriage or forced conversions that happened in the period as mentioned in the act.1 The citizenship of these women though was predominantly determined by their religion without considering other social factors, the question of citizenship of children born to abducted women loomed large in the minds of the lawmakers. The government passed a dictate that children born in Pakistan after the Partition had to be left behind by the mothers but ones born in India could be kept. In Kamlabehn's words, (a social worker involved in the recovery mission) "this was a complex problem. In Indian society, a child born to a Hindu mother by a Muslim father was hardly acceptable" (7). Bringing along such children would increase the chances of them ending up in orphanages as in Hindu society, they would be considered illegitimate. Therefore, the Indian government made a provision for women to bring their children to Jalandhar wherein the camps they could stay for fifteen days and decide if they wanted to part with them or not.

Special provisions were made for recovered pregnant women who could put up in the camps where they were guided to abortion and those in advanced stages would receive medical treatment and be kept there till they gave birth before sending them back to their families. (Menon and Bhasin 83) In a situation as this, where these women had to choose between social and familial acceptance and attachments, the recovery plans which were purposed to settle abducted women to where they 'rightfully belonged', made them question their identity and where they really belonged. The short stories Embrace and Banished amply exhibit the dilemma recovered women were faced with regarding their identities while they tried to reconcile themselves with their estranged family.

In "Embrace," Ramapada Chowdhury narrates the story of Sabita, who had been abducted earlier and is now back in her paternal home. What could be a story of a reunion of an abducted daughter with her mother and the rest of the family, is further complicated with the presence of an eight-month-old infant Sabita has brought along with her. On her arrival, Sabita is made aware that "many changes had occurred within this short span" (Chowdhury 339). Her father seems to be missing from the household for reasons undisclosed and her mother's attitude is somewhat changed who on her daughter's arrival only gave her a short welcoming call. Sabita's younger sister who initially chose silence when met with Sabita, soon after their mother leaves the site embraces the baby and lovingly converses with Sabita. Sabita's mother assumes the role of patriarch in the absence of her father. She brings about an air of uneasiness in Sabita who immediately takes her baby back from Kabita's arms when their mother arrives again. It is revealed that Sabita had been not gone for too long and when she was being brought back by the police, she protested questioning if her family would still have a place for her.

Now when she is back, she tries hard to make efforts to mingle with her family like the good old days putting up a smile even though she is tired from all the trauma she has been subjected to. However, she doubts her situation because the love and affection she should have received seem to have been deadened by the unfortunate impact her past life has cast upon her private space. Throughout the story, Sabita's mother repeatedly insists on washing up which can be perceived as an act of purification she wants her daughter to perform that she wished would help clean up her past and wash away all her 'sins'. The relationship between the mother and the daughter is noticeably uneasy where neither comfortably strike a real conversation with each other and Sabita too resorts to silence as "there was only one thing would remember or be reminded of – the memory of those humiliating days of the past" (340). The child becomes the sore point between the mother and daughter as Sabita's mother had been unable to accept Sabita's child. The child though born out of an act of violence, was for Sabita her flesh and blood whom she had brought along hoping to raise him for a brighter future. To her mother, the presence of the child makes it difficult for her to look at Sabita as an innocent daughter and acts as a reminder of her disgrace; she is unable to neither embrace her daughter or her grandchild. When admonished by her son for bathing in the evening, Sabita's mother says, "I have been holding and cuddling the baby the whole day...just because she has raised him in her lap, it does not make him a child of this family" (344). Sabita is subjected to a greater kind of damnation when she is ostracized by her mother in her own house proving that rehabilitation of women like Sabita is easier done on geographical maps than in the inner chambers of their house.

Jamila Hashimi's "Banished" is the story of a Muslim woman, Bibi, who lives with her Sikh abductor Gurpal in the village of Sangrao. She had been abducted by Gurpal while her family was moving after the Partition and he presented her before Bari Ma, his grandmother, as a serving maid. The story reveals that there were many 'bahus' like

Bibi in her village but "no one sang wedding songs to the beat of drums...hands were not decorated with henna, nor was my parting dressed in bridal red" (Hashimi 87). Bibi had however accepted this unusual marriage and continued living a life of a prisoner in Sangrao as Sita lived in exile. The banishment of the Sita of our story is but a long one. Her brother whom she hoped would come to rescue her hasn't arrived yet and now her daughter, Munni stands in between her past and her present. Her two sons born before Munni does not seem to bind her to the place as much as Munni does. Bibi seems to have grown her roots here post her daughter's birth and the fear of having to part with her if recovered, she hides when rescuers arrive in the village. Her daughter's future concerns her as she is not sure whether she will be taken back into her family along with her daughter and she says, "Where can I go...with my darkened fate? Munni stands in my way. She is the great distance that separates me from my own family" (93). To her, the world outside Sangrao seems to be a dark world of illusion with only uncertainty for her support. Bari Ma permits Bibi to step outside the house to the Dusshera fair accompanied by Gurpal and their children; it is ironic that our Sita follows her Ravan to see the Dusherra fair. Munni reminds her of the happy childhood she had spent with her father, mother and beloved brother whom she thinks of frequently.

The threshold of happy memories of her past with her family who have now been separated post the Partition, make her aware of her banishment with perhaps no hope for recovery in future as she doubtfully questions the government's plans for the rehabilitation of abducted women- "Repatriate them to what country? Where? To whom?" (100) The situation of Sabita and Bibi are thus alike, they are both confronted with the question of identity and belongingness. Sabita cannot overcome her fate of being seen as a stakeholder of honour and a birthing citizen who now stands corrupted having brought along her illegitimate child. By the laws of the government, she neither belongs to her abductor nor does the social dictates allow her to reconcile with her family where she is forcefully returned to and is therefore subjected to banishment in her own house. Bibi on the other hand, due to lack of a promise of a secured future away in a nation now unknown to her, chooses a life of eternal banishment with her abductor. For both Sabita and Bibi, their memories are their only safe refuge as their realities have changed now. Both are caught in a state of perpetual homelessness and their narrative problematizes the concept of nation and identity in the post Partition era.

Conclusion

The 1947 Partition which brought along multifarious violence, affected the women population sorely. Abduction during the communal riots was the most common form of violence that was inflicted upon women in the history of the Partition of the Indian subcontinent compelling the governments of India and Pakistan to come to a consensus and formulate recovery missions and parliamentary acts to bring back women to their original place of inhabitance and give them a free environment. This dissertation has sought to demonstrate that the corrective measures introduced by both the governments of India and Pakistan as altruistic policies on the account of abductions, led to a form of displacement for such women that they could never relocate themselves in the folds of society.

To prove this argument, I have considered the short stories- The Stricken Daughter, Embrace, Lajwanti and

Banished that encapsulate the experiences of dislocated women caught in the dictates of the governmental policies further amplifying the trauma they had once already undergone. The likes of the protagonists of the above-mentioned stories can never be restored in the true sense of the term as the government only pursued to determine their citizenship based on their communal and religious identities not realizing that their experiences had changed them; they may have been restored to their original families but they could never be restored to their pre-abducted state of mind making their rehabilitation difficult at a psychological level. Menon and Bhasin in their essay point out that the recovery operations were "implemented within the parameters of two overriding factors; first the relationship of the Indian state with Pakistan and second, its assumption of the role of 'parens patriae vis-à-vis the women who had been abducted" (8).

The recovery of these women took place under the assumption that all of them were abducted by members of the rival community in the enemy land. Such a presumption took away the agencies of such women to determine their fate, denying them their fundamental rights as citizens and silencing their voices. This also brings to the forefront and problematizes the patriarchal mindset of the Indian state that manipulated the rescue missions into reclaiming their Hindu women and restoring them to the Hindu fold to compensate their egos and redeem themselves from the humiliation of having failed to protect them in the first place. The orthodox Hindu system of marriage and family was overlooked completely when considering the rehabilitation of abducted women as these women would often be forcefully married, converted and impregnated by their abductors. Upon her return, her sexuality was questioned, her honour was now tainted making it difficult for her to get accepted in her family and her child was considered illegitimate.

Acts and policies which can be charted on papers and function at the legal front, cannot be mapped onto the complex human relations and value systems of a community. Though the motive of the abductors and the Indian government was separate, they both proved to be detrimental for women and the government failed to deliver the "izzat" and the free environment they had promised to these women while relocating them to India. These women were left to their own fate hence where they found themselves in a state where they faced resistance both in the inner and outer spheres of their existence. Therefore, even though The Abducted Persons (Recovery and Restoration) Act of 1949, yielded excellent statistical results in recovering abducted women across the border, it failed to restore them and ended up further displacing them.

The silence that society forced upon abducted victims because of the shame that is associated with it has led to very little documentation of the real experiences of the victims themselves post their recovery. The majority of it is available documented only in the voices of social workers associated with the recovery making literature a reliable source to trace the fate of these women and conduct a survey to determine the success of such policies. First-hand narrations would further reveal the destiny of children accompanying their abducted mothers to their legal homelands which remains an area that could be researched further to determine if these corrective measures proved to be beneficial at all.

Works Cited

An Epic Unwritten: The Penguin Book of Partition Stories. Ed. Muhammad Umar Memon. Trans. Muhammad Umar Memon. New Delhi: Penguin India, 2010. Print.

---. Hashimi, Jamila. "Banished." *An Epic Unwritten: The Penguin Book of Partition Stories.* New Delhi: Penguin India, 2010. 85-103. Print.

---. Bedi, Rajinder Singh. "Banished." *An Epic Unwritten: The Penguin Book of Partition Stories.* New Delhi: Penguin India, 2010. 15-29. Print.

Bengal Partition Stories: An Unclosed Chapter. Ed. Bashabi Fraser. London: Anthem, 2008. Print.

---. Chowdhury, Ramapada. "The Stricken Daughter." Trans. Sheila Sengupta. *Bengal Partition Stories: An Unclosed Chapter.* London: Anthem, 2008. 323-38. Print.

---. Chowdhury, Ramapada. "Embrace." Trans. Sheila Sengupta. *Bengal Partition Stories: An Unclosed Chapter.* London: Anthem, 2008. 339-44. Print.

Bombay High Court Website. "Abducted Persons (Recovery and Restoration) Act, 1949", Web. <https://bombayhighcourt.nic.in/libweb/actc/1949.65.pdf>. Accessed 7 Mar.2021.

Bhalla, Guneeta Singh. "The Partition Archive", 2010. Web.< https://in.1947partitionarchive.org/> Accessed 24 Mar. 2021.

Butalia, Urvashi. The Other Side of Silence Voices from the Partition of India. New Delhi: Penguin Books India, 1998. Print.

---. "Questions of Sexuality and Citizenship during Partition." Embodiment: Essays on Gender and Identity. Ed. Meenakshi Thapan. New Delhi: Oxford University Press, 1997: 90-106.

Dey, Arunima "Violence against Women during the Partition of India: Interpreting Women and their Bodies in the Context of Ethnic Genocide". Spain: Revista de Filologia Inglesa 37, 2016.

Menon, Ritu and Kamla Bhasin. *Borders and Boundaries: Women in India's Partition.* New Delhi: Kali for Women, 1998. Print.

---. Menon, Ritu, and Kamla Bhasin. "Recovery, Rupture, Resistance: Indian State and Abduction of Women during Partition." Economic and Political Weekly, vol. 28, no. 17, 1993, pp. WS2–WS11. JSTOR, < www.jstor.org/stable/4399640>. Accessed 7 Mar. 2021.

CHAPTER III

THE SURVIVOR OF HEYDAY: FLAVOUR OF ECOFEMINISM IN THE HANDMAID'S TALE

Joshna Francis

Assistant Professor on Contract

Bhavan's College of Arts & Commerce

Kakkanad, Ernakulam.

Abstract

The paper titled "The Survivor of Heyday: Flavour of Ecofeminism in *The Handmaid's Tale*," explores the consequences of environmental degradation on women. The topicmainly focuses on analysing the Eco feministic elements in Margaret Atwood's *The Handmaid's Tale*, which is typically a dystopian novel, presents a gloomy future vision and repression of women leadingdown to the reduction of their image to the child-producing machine in a totalitarian, theocratic state.

The traditional notion of a connection between women and nature is a relic of patriarchy - an instrument of oppression- which should be allowed to wither away. Eco feminists linked environmental degradation with patriarchal culture and believed that a social structure based upon the principles of complete equality and the absence of all oppression would prevent the destruction of human beings and the planet. When men focus on the strength and power that technology and civilization bring to them, females hope to find harmony, equality, wholeness and mutual benefit by getting close to nature which shows nature's healing power upon women and the closeness between women and nature. Thus, there is a need for an ecological revolution led by women, which would establish equality of gender relations and bring an end to the power of one group over another- including the domination of humans over nature.

By taking females as the leading characters and environmental crisis in its background, Atwood expertly combines in *The Handmaid's Tale* the dual oppression of nature and women that exists in the Republic of Gilead. She points out that the injustice meted out against women and nature is alike and no attempt to liberate women will be successful without an equal attempt to liberate nature. This article based on ecofeminism focuses on analysing the ecological imbalance which leads to the deterioration of women which results in the marginalization and identity crisis challenging them both mentally and physically endangering their lives.

Keywords: Ecofeminism, patriarchy, marginalization.

● ● ●

The Survivor of Heyday: Flavour of Ecofeminism in *The Handmaid's Tale*

One of the crucial problems that we face today is the degradation of land and the environment and its consequences on human life and existence. The uncanny power and splendour of nature have become only a mere dream for the young minds of this modern world. To live a peaceful and balanced human life on this earth, the preservation of the environment is necessary. Often women can be identified with nature. Throughout history nature is portrayed as feminine – their reproductive capacities make women closer to nature than men. Both women and nature are life-sustaining and resource giving but their role is often neglected and sidelined in society. Oppression has been an issue that has affected human life for a very long time. The power that is levelled upon nature causes the same harm that is similar to that resulting from the oppression of women. Senseless use of interventions, modern industrial developments and technology, the greenhouse gas emissions, degradation of water resources, deforestation, senseless use of pesticides, electronic wastes, radio nuclei and their emissions etc are some of the issues that result in the sterility of nature and the sterility of society comes from men's hostility towards women. Women are hurt most as they suffer double oppression of patriarchy, education, race and poverty. It is in this context, that the term Ecofeminism becomes highly relevant.

The term Ecofeminism was first coined by French Feminist Françoise d' Eaubonne in 1974; who has called upon women to lead an ecological revolution to save earth from destruction. Ecofeminism is a concept that attempts to study the exploitation of nature as similar to the exploitation of women and visualizes a new humanism that resists and subverts all political hierarchies, social and economic structures that oppress women and all that do harm to organic life as a whole. It does not seek equality with men as such but aims for the liberation of women as women. Ecofeminists believe in the interconnectedness of things and explore how male domination of women and domination of nature are interconnected. The exploitation of the earth and of the women's bodies goes hand in hand, under the system of male dominance. The commercialization of natural resources has made necessary the application of technology in seed production and plant raising. Like nature, the female body is seen as a resource to be colonized and commercialized. The new developments in biotechnology, genetic engineering and reproductive technologies have affected the rhythms and regenerative capacities of women and nature. Although scholars disagree as to whether patriarchal social structures were preceded by matriarchal forms, it is certain that virtually all primitive peoples worshipped a mother goddess. Recognized as the source of life and thus the embodiment of fertility, the mother eventually came to represent the archetypal feminine. Erich Neumann describes this development in his study of the Great Mother archetype:

It is only relatively late in the history of mankind that we find the

Archetypal Feminine designated as Magna Mater. But it was worshipped

and portrayed many thousands of years before the appearance of the

term.... [A] wreath of symbolic images, however, surrounds not only

one figure but a great number of figures, of Great Mothers who, as

goddess and fairies, female demons and nymphs, friendly and unfriendly,

manifest the one Great Unknown, the Great Mother as the central aspect

of the Archetypal Feminine, in the rites and myths, the religion and

legends, of mankind. (Finney 145)

The archetype of the mother or Great Mother has continued to captivate the human imagination in a wide variety of incarnations. What might be called the cult of the mother reached the height of its influence in the nineteenth century, when the rigid sexual division of spheres produced an isolated domestic realm over which the mother reigned supreme; as Nancy Chodorow and Susan Contratto observe, "At a time when everyone's life was being affected by the frenzied growth of developing industrial capitalism, somehow mothers were seen as having total control and unlimited power in the creation of their children" (Finney 146). In larger social terms, however, maternity and mother-dominated child-raising are potentially the roots of female oppression, in so far as they can serve to confine the women to the home.

In *The Handmaid's Tale* Margret Atwood depicts the adverse effect of environmental degradation on the life of women. Gilead, the biblically-inflected nation Atwood imagines is a totalitarian country that features taming and ruling of females. The natural world is denatured by man in the Republic of Gilead and pollution of the environment has resulted in sterility and deformity of the offspring. The consequences of this hazard are suffered by the women in Gilead. They are triply marginalized. The first marginalization is that the women are marginalized in their own nation, the second is gender marginalization which is through the men of Gilead, and the third is the class marginalization which is by- women on women. That is, the women with good social respect and order gain their power over the handmaids. Women with viable ovaries are forced into a submissive position and are used for procreation and to bear children for childless Commanders and to act as handmaids. When a woman consents to sell her reproductive services to a married infertile couple, her consent is about as genuine as the "consent" a woman gives when she sells her sexual services to a client; and when society encourages a woman to rent her womb, it comes dangerously close to dehumanizing reproduction by turning it into a mode of commodity production.

In this new regime, the word 'sterile' is banned. There are only women who are fruitful and fruitless. The protagonist Offered is one of the many handmaids in Gilead. The handmaids are dressed uniformly and are given no name or identity. They are known only after the Commanders with whom they have to perform the impregnation ceremony, in a ritualistic and objective manner. Their very names are merely devices used to devote to whom they belong; broken up into their component parts, it is clear that the women are "Of Fred", "Of Warren", "Of Glen, "Of Charles", etc. These handmaids who are degraded to the level of mere reproductive beings are desexed, dehumanized and are forbidden choice and desire. They are not supposed to think and feel. Thus Offered says: "I try not to think too much. Like other things now, thought must be rationed" (Atwood 17).

The only emotion that they are enforced to bear is fear. They have lost their identity and the heroine who is depicted as a passive creature in this novel sometimes seems to live in her past. She thinks of her job, her life as an emancipated woman free-roaming throughout the city, visiting clubs and her affair with a married man (Luke), who for her divorced his wife and remarried her, their happy life resulting in a child touched her feelings where now she is in a state who has lost their track. She had seen them when they are captured by the Eye- the police force of Gilead and was till then left unaware of their path. With the loss of all her identity and even her name she now realized herself as a handmaid - the property of someone, which shows that she is not even sure of whose property. The only attitude they are supposed to adopt is passivity.

Women whose wombs are not viable in terms of childbirth are not really women at all, according to the founders of this theocracy. If they fail to produce a child within the three chances given to them, they will be declared as un-women and exiled to the colonies, where they clean toxic waste and act as slave labourers. Such narrow-minded treatment reveals the Republic of Gilead's complete disregard for the actual lives and personalities of its female citizens. Essentially, men raped the Earth until it could not be raped any longer, so they turned their attention to raping women instead. By having the Republic of Gilead use the environment as a means of attaining power, Atwood seems to be making an ecofeminist critique of both the questionable practices of companies that deal with chemicals, oil, nuclear products, and other potentially hazardous materials and the external influences which politicians use to bolster their support and solidify their power.

The act of begetting a child for the upper-class couple is called an assignment in the Republic. Often the offspring born were deformed ones due to ecological degeneration. The effect is reflected in the animal world also. Fishes have become extinct like whales. In the novel, there are frequent references to animals, plants, smells and other objects typically associated with nature. The handmaids are told to think of themselves as seeds – seeds and fruits are associated with manipulated, no natural reproduction. Nature in Gilead is thus seen as a justification for male sexual dominance and female oppression. In the novel, the natural creatures and phenomena are seen as the incarnation of females and the product of civilization such as guns, cars and books are the incarnation of males.

The society of Gilead is built on the biblical notion that men are more important than women. What is most provocative is that, in the name of religion, in the name of the Bible much crime and sin are perpetrated in society arrogantly converting laws for their advantage. Women are punished because since biblical times they are considered transgressors. So they are made subservient to their husbands. "For Adam was first formed, then Eve. And Adam was not deceived but the woman being deceived was in the transgression. Notwithstanding she shall be saved by childbearing" (233). Women are made to believe that they are unholy and unclean if they don't serve the purpose of their creation. Women are seen as still perpetrating Eve's vices persistently by Gileadian theocracy, the so-called state-in-religion or religion-in-state, so they are not trusted with any authority or power.

Gilead creates an official vocabulary that ignores and warps reality in order to serve the needs of the new society's elite. Women in Gilead are not permitted to read, hold jobs, or have money. They are denied books, paper, and pens; even to scribble is a clandestine venture. Their arms and legs are chapped off if they are caught reading or writing; as such things are ruthlessly considered inessential for reproduction. Having made it illegal for women to hold jobs, Gilead creates a system of titles. Whereas men are defined by their military rank, women are defined solely by their gender roles as Wives, Handmaids, or Marthas. There are prescribed greetings for personal encounters, and to fail to offer the correct greeting is to fall under suspicion of disloyalty. In the novel, there is a ceremony once a month where the handmaids are to sleep with their assigned Commanders in an attempt to become pregnant. Women are compared to prize pigs, which is a form of oppression because this dehumanizes them. Pigs are regarded as lazy, brainless, and helpless animals. By comparing Offred to a pig, Atwood depicts how men in Gilead view women. The handmaids are locked in their room in their Commander's house and wait around on the day of the ceremony and for the men. They are taken care of very meticulously on the day of the ceremony as if they cannot take care of themselves. This shows that society views these women as clueless and helpless.

Indoctrination was a strong and effective tool used by the Republic of Gilead to enforce its control over the subjugated female population throughout the story. It was especially prevalent in the Rachael and Leah Re-Education Center (also known as the Red Centers) which Offered, Moira and Janine attended. It has its origin from the biblical story of Rachael and Leah who gave their Handmaids to their husbands in order to keep their position intact. At the Red centre, the Aunts are entrusted with the crucial duty of training the Handmaids because they rank among the most powerful female agents of the patriarchal order.

The handlers in the Red Center managed to turn women against themselves and their own beliefs. The behaviour of women in the Red Center was restricted in that their daily lives were strictly scheduled and their ability to talk, walk, read and even to use the bathroom was limited; similarly, their beliefs were ideologically restricted (and thus, altered) in that much of what they previously believed was depicted as evil and unhealthy. Within the confines of the Red Center, abuse is predominately psychological. Humiliation is a favourite technique of the Aunts. Janine, another Handmaid-in-training, repeatedly suffers public humiliation. According to the Aunts as spokeswomen for the patriarchy of Gilead, rape and other forms of sexual and domestic violence are consequences of women possessing sexual freedom and leading men on. If psychological avenues are unsuccessful, the Aunts use physical violence to control the women in charge.

The theocratic government ruling over the Republic of Gilead utilizes strange hybridity of science and religion to rule the lives of its population of Handmaids. Offred is brutally awakened to the hypocrisy and hollowness of the whole system when she is confronted with the fact that the Commanders use the services of prostitutes, thus circumventing and subverting a system that they themselves helped to establish. From an ecofeminist perspective, this is highly exploitative. By night, they are exploiting the same women whom they ostensibly hold on a pedestal by day. The act of taking a supposedly – sacred woman and thoroughly debasing her reflects a distinct lack of conviction and lack of true belief; however, it is ultimately indicative of a love of having power and control over others, which seems to have been the actual reason for the implementation of the Republic of Gilead, to begin with.

Offred's freedom, like the freedom of all women, is completely restricted. She can leave the house only on shopping trips, the door to her room cannot be completely shut, and the Eyes, Gilead's secret police force, watch her every public move. Women can be arrested or shot for being alone in public or for conversing with one another about anything other than the daily tasks assigned to them. Offred is allowed to attend a few social functions, such as Birth Day celebrations and women's Salvaging; these activities reinforce her role in Gilead. The Birth Day celebrations remind Offered of her duty to her household, her Commander, and her country. The Salvagings remind

Offred of the consequence of any failure to follow the rules and regulations of Gilead. All of her other activities are designed to keep her body in prime reproductive health: daily exercise on the floor of her bedroom, daily walks to the market, and her scheduled baths.

Sexual violence, particularly against women, pervades *The Handmaid's Tale*. This is most evident in the Ceremony which compels Handmaids to have sex with their Commanders. The patriarchy has institutionalized adultery, under the guise of reproduction. Both Wife and Handmaid/Mistress are required co-habit the house and must collaborate in the procreative mission of the household. Conception is the focus of family life in Gilead. The Ceremony is a socially condoned ménage a Trois. Offred reflects that "it has nothing to do with passion or love or romance or any of those notions we used to titillate ourselves with. It has nothing to do with sexual desire, at least for me, and certainly not for Serena" (94).

Bonding with her Commander allowed Offred to relieve at least a portion of the mind-numbingly monotonous boredom which dominated the majority of her day-to-day existence. It also afforded her the opportunity to learn various bits and pieces of news about the current state of affairs in the country of which she would have otherwise remained ignorant. Ironically, even the rallying cry of resistance used against the patriarchal oppressors by Offred and her predecessor, Nolite te bastardes carborundorum (a bastardized Latin phrase meaning "don't let the bastards grind you down"), was learned from the man who represented and enforced that oppression.

Neither Offred nor her Commander found the ceremony pleasurable. It is possible that the founders of the Republic of Gilead were primarily concerned with reproduction and procreation when they decided to sexually enslave a substantial portion of the female population; however, the need for psychological power and control is also a plausible reason for their hostile take-over of the country and sexual enslavement of women.

Both women and nature suffer under patriarchal domination and are treated as objects to be controlled, subdued, consumed, exploited and tamed. In order to know their secret, to control and tame them, men of Science struggled to subdue nature and women and thus women, as well as nature, came to be dominated, controlled and exploited. And women become scapegoats for those exploiting the environment. The master-slave role which marks man's relation with nature is replicated in man's relationship with a woman.

The Handmaid's Tale is a good model of a docile society with the complexities of body image. Atwood uses the female body as a treatment of the mind/ body concept and analyses the way, in which her character responds to, and resists its destructive effects. The bodies of women in Atwood is novel as the handmaids are severely scrutinized to show how a body can be docile. The female bodies in the novel are controlled both spatially and physically and by all means docile. As all the Handmaids are the object of surveillance, their movements, bodies, minds and attitudes are the targets of others, including men of different social categories, Commanders, Guardians, Eyes and women as Aunts, Wives, even the Handmaids' that unwillingly support the system of surveillance by spying on each other.

Another of the novel's most important themes is the exploration of the relationship between women. It comprises Offred's record of life within the matriarchy of Gilead. As she performs her rote duties, under the strict system of female control, she struggles to come to terms with her multiple losses: culture, family, identity, agency, and, most importantly, companionship. Though the Aunts insist that a household is a place of camaraderie, the domestic hierarchy thrives on mutual dislike and disapproval.

In Gilead, females were turned against, one another. They were often envious of one another instead of being supportive. The Economies resented the Handmaids because of what they perceived to be a pampered, carefree way of life; in fact, almost all of the other female castes seemed to resent the Handmaids. The Wives consider the Handmaids distasteful. During a Birth Day visit, the Commander's Wife makes the following comment to her friends, "Little whores, all of them, but still you can't be choosy. You take what they hand out, right, girls?" (125). The Wives resented them for stealing away the sexual attention of their husbands, and the Marthas resented them because of the responsibilities and chores that taking care of the Handmaids entailed. The Handmaids are personal affronts to the Wives; they are continual reminders of the Wives' failures to conceive.

The Wives attitude towards the Handmaids recalls the biblical characters in the Old Testament namely- Sarah and Hagar. The Handmaids are treated as the logs of wood by the women in power. This can be viewed when the Commander's wife Serena asks Offred to have sex with her chauffeur Nick secretly and pass the child off as the Commander's. Serena promises to bring Offred a picture of her daughter if she sleeps with Nick, and Offered realizes that Serena has always known the whereabouts of Offred's daughter. Not only has she cruelly concealed this knowledge she is willing to exploit Offred's loss of a child in order to get an infant of her own. Serena's lack of sympathy makes her the perfect figure for Gilead's social order, which relies on the willingness of women to oppress other women. She is a cruel selfish woman, and Atwood implies that such women are the glue that binds Gilead. Ultimately, Serena is able to subdue her, by using Offred's maternal affection as a cheap tool to carry out her evil plans.

Mother Earth is seen as the vitality which generates growth and germination in her maternal womb. According to Madhu Khanna, the Atharva Veda espouses a strategy with a sensitive attitude towards the integrity and stability of the biotic community. The following hymn (where the earth is invoked with a feeling of great humility) is offered as an example:

Whatever, I dig of you, O Earth,

May that grow quickly upon you,

O Pure One, may my thrust never pierce thy

Vital points, Thy heart (Datar 116)

Like nature, here a mother scarifies herself for her child. According to William Wordsworth, it is necessary for sustaining the connection between the individual and nature. In "Tintern Abbey," Wordsworth writes – "Nature never did betray/ The heart that loved her" (lines 123-124). The beauty of nature is like a mother: it can provide peace, comfort, or suffering for its children. This unconditional love is exploited by the people for their own sake.

It is the fear for herself and for her lover and child that keeps Offred passive in the beginning. But her emotions and vitality are not to be suppressed for long after the ceremonial fertilization, she aches for Luke, her lover. Her developing awareness of herself as a victimized woman kindles in her the desire to subvert the pervasive canons of Gilead. Her secret affair with Nick and with the underground Network-May Day, meant for rescuing women and conducting sabotage are the results of that. Eventually, she is saved from Gilead by Nick, though the readers are not sure whether this freedom is everlasting or not. They present the mission of Gilead as: "Women united for a common end! Helping one another in their daily chores as they walk the path of life together, each performing her appointed task" (171).

The Handmaid's Tale ends on a note of disappointing ambiguity. The readers are left with more questions than answers as Offred steps up "into the darkness within; or else the light" (307). Did Offred escape? What became of her? Did she devote herself to the resistance? The text fails to answer the questions. The novel emphasizes sympathizing with Offred and judging Gilead as tyrannical and oppressive.

In *The Handmaid's Tale*, Atwood delineates a story of victimization, exploitation of female sex for procreation, gender politics of patriarchy reducing women to the point of zero, power politics of the postmodern world and consumer society playing a game with women's lives through subversive rules and religious dogmas to thwart the women's lives in search of survival. By setting the novel in the near future, Atwood envisions a future that would rectify all the evils against women by the male-dominated society, at the same time, depicts a picture of gruesome contemporary scenario where the situation with regard to women is getting aggravated beyond hope and redemption.

This novel – *The Handmaid's Tale* gives a wake-up call and alerts the readers that misuse and abuse of nature and technology militate against a genuinely good quality of life. The abysmal world that Atwood paints make readers cognizant of the fact that they cannot have excessive chemical products or toxic fast foods without risking clean air and good health. This danger to nature will surely lead to the struggle for identity of the population living in this polluted world. Thus, it can be considered that every aspect of environmental degradation, destruction and abuse of nature will translate itself into a serious menace to the life of future generations. This cautionary futuristic novel reveals Atwood's ability to peer behind the curtains into some of the darkest and most disturbing truths about environmental hazards that pose a perilous threat to the world which challenges the identity of the human race which is competing with it.

Works Cited

Primary Source

Atwood, Margaret. *The Handmaid's Tale.* London: Vintage, 1996.

Secondary Source

Abrams, M.H. *A Glossary of Literary Terms and Literary Theory.* New Delhi: Thomson Learning, 2008.

Datar, Chhaya. *Ecofeminism Revisited: Introduction to the Discourse.* Jaipur: Rawat. 2011.

Finney, Gail. *Women in Modern Drama.* New York: Cornell UP, 1991.

Garrard, Greg. *Ecocriticism.* 2nd ed. Oxon: Routledge, 2013.

Howells, Coral Ann. *Margaret Atwood.* New York: Palgrave MacMillan, 2005.

Wordsworth, William. "Tintern Abbey." *Twenty-Four Poems.* Ed. Gigy Joseph. Changanacherry: Lilly, 2013.

Sharma, P. D. *Ecology and Environment.* 7th ed. Meerut: Rastogi, 2006.

Bio- Note

Ms. Joshna Francis holds a Master's in English from St. Albert's College, Ernakulam and resides in Fort Kochi. She has completed B.Ed. in English and has qualified SET. She is in the 6th year of her teaching career. She joined Bhavan's College of Arts & Commerce, as Assistant Professor on contract in the Department of English in 2016.

WILLING SUSPENSION OF DISBELIEF: A MYTHICAL JOURNEY THROUGH NJAN GANDHARVAN AND TUMBHAD

Neethu Anna Tharakan

Assistant Professor, Department of English

Mar Ivanios College, Trivandrum.

Abstract

A film or a movie can be defined as a series of still images which when shown on the screen create the illusion of moving images. The film plays an important role in concretizing what is abstract. The genres of the film include thrillers, adventures, supernatural, films related to myth and folktales, music, romance, fantasy, horrors etc. Among these, the most significant are mythological films with the fantastic narrations of ancient stories. *Njan Gandharvan* the 1991 romantic fantasy directed by P Padmarajan is a brilliant retelling of the old Gandharva myth. Gandharvas were singers from heaven and their visits to earth are believed to cast spells on maidens. The director had a special liking for fantasy. *Tumbhad* the 2018 Hindi language horror film directed by Rahi Anil Barve is based on the myth of Hastar, the fallen God-turned demon. The myths portrayed in the two movies were dealt with an attitude of awe and fear by traditional Hindus. The purpose of this paper is to demonstrate how these two films - one old and one new - weave together two genres of literature, myths and folktales, through the concept of "Willing Suspension of Disbelief", a term coined by the great romantic poet Samuel Taylor Coleridge.

Keywords: concretizing, myth and folktales

Willing Suspension of Disbelief: A Mythical Journey through Njan Gandharvan and Tumbhad

There has always been a relationship between literature and film since both have a common medium-narration. In films dialogues, noise, sounds, scenes, settings and music help to manipulate the emotions and the expressive nature of the story. Just like films literature has been used as a medium to voice the thoughts, attitudes, beliefs and emotions of the human world. A character in literature and an actor in a movie are identified as the same. For example, in a novel, if the character is shown to play the piano, in the film we see the actor playing the same. Indian cinema like other film industries reflects the country's political, economic, social and cultural aspects. It aids in understanding the soul of India. Films open a most useful window onto the culture of a country and according to Raymond Williams culture is ' a whole way of life'.K.Moti Gokulsing and Wimal Dissanayake in their book "Indian Popular Cinema-a narrative of cultural change" speaks in detail about the culture and how it forms the subjects of various Indian films.

India is a religiously plural society. Religion is a system having various beliefs, practices, texts, or spiritual elements which are connected with God or gods. It is a universal phenomenon. It acts as the strongest means of social control. The term religion can have different meanings as it varies from person to person. Folk tales and myths are associated with religion. They help in connecting religion and human beings. In India, the majority of its people are Hindus. Religious authority is widely diffused in the Hindu world. Right from the traditional times' myths and folktales remained as part of Indian culture mainly with the Hindu religion. The same can be seen in books as well. Mythological films constitute a very important segment of Indian popular cinema. They have their roots in the ancient past in that they deal with characters and events often inscribed in epics and scriptures. They depict the action of gods, demons, and supernatural powers.

Myths and folktales always made an everlasting imprint in the mind of the audience. Myth can be the story of gods or heroes which is commonly held as a belief. People generally hold myth as a true account of the remote past. Certain myths are tied to religion as well .'Gandharva' is one such myth. This myth is commonly held as a belief by the Hindus. 'Gandharva' (also termed as a male version of Yakshi) is a Sanskrit term that means 'fragrance'. They are often attracted by the music, wilderness and beautiful women. In the movie *Tumbhad* the director conveys the idea that all deities of the Hindu religion were the sons and daughters of the Goddess of plenty. The title of the movie is a fictional place. It is somewhat close to the mountainous region of Pune. In the film, Hastar is the central character. Though not mentioned in any texts, many people believe that he is a fictional God.

As per the movie, the Goddess of plenty gave birth to sixteen core gods and Hastar was the first one. But he was very greedy. He tried to snatch all the wealth by himself. Fed up with this his siblings attacked him and shattered him into pieces. But before turning into dust the Goddess of plenty, out of sympathy imprisoned him in her womb, but on one condition that people never worship him. But unfortunately, as the film says people build a temple for him and started worshipping him. P Padmarajan's movie

Njan Gandharvan mingles two genres – romance and myth. The director introduces Bhama the heroine and Devan, the 'Gandharva'. The audience is made to travel into the world of awe, imagination and creativity. The love between a mortal woman and a 'Gandharva' enhances the supernatural aura of the movie. Visually seductive the movie creates a world where the audience finds it difficult to determine where reality ends and fantasy begins.

However, people tend to believe in spirits, sorceresses, demons, Gandharvas, etc., even though they know they do not exist to some extent because both films and literature have been used to carry ideas or beliefs about the supernatural and its relationship to humanity. Many writers and filmmakers adopted the theme of myths and folktales because it makes the viewers and readers travel into a world of make-believe thereby temporarily accepting the events portrayed. Coleridge's phrase 'Willing Suspension of Disbelief suits well in the present context. In his seminal work "Biographia Litereria" Coleridge writes:

The poet does not require to be awake and believe. He solicits us

only to yield ourselves to a dream and this, too, with our eyes

open, and with our judgement perdue behind the curtain really to

awaken us at the first motion of our will: and meantime only, not to disbelieve. (Coleridge 87)

As we look back at the evolution of art forms such as drama, poetry, painting, fiction, and even film, we can see that religious concepts and myths have always found a place. Most of the myths associated with religion has been passed on from one generation to another. *Njan Gandharva* is a 1991 film and *Tumbhad* s somewhat recent. These movies continue to be enjoyed by both older and younger generations. The plot of *Njan Gandharvan* is not complicated. They are essentially simple and little effort is made to portray complex characters. Just like a magician the director creates a world of make-believe and presents before the vast audience. Stories related to myth are told and presented in such a way that we are forced to believe the improbable and supernatural. In addition to elevating the movie to greater heights, music also accentuates its romantic tone. The flow of emotions between Bhama and Devan appears to be eternal. Both of them are in deeply love with each other forgetting the fact that Devan is a 'Gandharva'. According to the rule of heaven, Gandharvas are not supposed to spend too much time in the mortal world. They have to return to heaven after seducing the maiden. But unlike other Gandharvas, Devan cannot leave Bhama alone. Bhama on the other hand doesn't want Devan to suffer because of her. She is ready to offer herself to save him.

The vast majority of Indian films look for morals and the power of God to correct injustice. The language used in such films will be more close to religious sentiments and convictions. In the contest between justice and injustice, light and darkness, wisdom and ignorance, the force of light, justice and wisdom wins. Certain films related to myth presents the conflict between human greed and human need. Man always longs for more and more. The real contest is between greed and need. The film *Tumbhad* opens with a meaningful quote from Mahatma Gandhi. He states that "the world has enough for everyone's need, but not for everyone's greed". The whole plot of the story revolves around the same idea. We can see the Tumbhad village that never stops raining. A small creepy statue of

Hastar can also be seen at times. He is shown holding a single gold coin in his hands. As per the movies the demon God is not named for it brings misfortune to the village. Sohum Shah as Vinayak is shown as a greedy man who tries to snatch away the treasure guarded by Hastar. Whoever enters the mansion for the gold is attacked by unseen forces. Towards the end, we can see Vinayak burning with rage as he challenges the unseen Hastar. Though a horror movie it essentially conveys a message. It exposes the dark side of the human mind.

Incidents and happenings depicted in these two movies are completely divorced from reality. In order to enjoy the movie, we have to suspend our faculty of disbelief and transcend the thin veneer of it, delving deep into the very spirit of the movie which in Coleridgean parlance is 'willing suspension of disbelief. Every literary creation is mysterious, whether it be drama, movie novel or poetry. Movies related to myths and folktales have a sort of connection with the human psyche. Sometimes they connect us to our own inner process. Such films are quite thrilling as well. At the same time, these genres often set a universe without any people or location from real life. In *Njan Gandharvan* Padmarajan mixes two genres: romance and myth. He makes the spectators travel into a world of imagination and reality. Certain scenes are visually seductive. On the other hand in *Tumbhad* the horror world of Hastar is brought out. We can see the protagonist fall into the bottomless pit of greed thereby making him give up his life. At times the film makes us think about what is right and wrong.

Every literary creation is mysterious, whether it be film, drama, novel or poetry. A movie, like literature, takes the audience to the ultimate aesthetic bliss. The great literary figure William Shakespeare in his seminal work *A Midsummer Night's Dream* describes a poet:

> The poet's eye in a fine frenzy rolling, doth glance
> From heauen to earth, from earth to heauen.
> And as imagination bodies forth the forms of things
> Vnknowne; the Poet's pen turns them to shapes,
> And giues to aire nothing a local habitation,
> And a name. (5.1.14-19)

In traditional times myths were transmitted orally. But the film industry has aided filmmakers to transmit myths to large audiences because films are where art and technology meet. Virtual technologies and digital images are advancing at a fast pace these days, and many filmmakers use myths and folktales to attract a younger audience. People attribute many names to various mythical figures. Some of the common names are 'Odiyan', 'Yakshi', 'Gandharva', 'Chattan' etc. In a society where such myths are told, it is usually regarded as a true account of the remote past.

V. S. Sethuraman in "Indian Aesthetics an Introduction" has given an account of emotions that stir the mind of the people. An artist or a writer does not do this because he has thought long over but because he is inspired. It is a spontaneous overflow of powerful feelings. Films, just like literature appeals to emotions. Certain films related to myths elevates the heart of the spectators. On the stage, the actor plays his role well. The character played by the actor makes an everlasting imprint in the mind of the audience. Even if years pass by it remains in our hearts. There are a good number of films associated with myths and folktales in all film industries. As far as Mollywood is concerned "Njan Gandharvan" still holds a greater place. It's P.Padmarajan's last movie. It is a film filled with creativity and magical moments. Padmarajan enriches the movie with his imagination and creativity. He tried to explore the different facets of human life. The novelty of themes was his hallmark. Some of his major works are "Toovanathumbikal", "Deshadanaliki Karayarilla", "Namukkuparkan Munthiri Toopukal" and *Njan Gandharva*. Rahi Anil Barve worked predominantly in Bollywood. His major film to hit theatre was *Tumbhad*. It took almost eight years to complete the movie. Even though he faced my hardships he brought out a movie which was a great success.

Many recent films continued the trend of mixing traditional mythology to create the plot for modern readers. Such additions add meaning and value to the stories for the present audience. Myths are an ongoing social practice within every society. Even before the printed literature myths and folktales existed in spoken forms. Using these themes as a hook to draw in a large audience is common in all film industries. The task is challenging as well. They have to treat characters that are incredible and improbable. Under normal circumstances, people won't believe. What is needed is a willing suspension of disbelief so that at least for a few moments we would believe for a few moments what is essentially improbable and incredible. The treatment of myths and folktales in movies and literature is such that it sends the judgements of the readers to sleep, so as to say so that they would peruse the work of art with supreme delight.

Works Cited

Coleridge, Samuel Taylor. "Biographia Literaria". New York. Oxford University Press, 1817.

Gokulsing, K.Moti and Wimal Dissanayake. "Indian Popular Cinema- a narrative of cultural change". Orient Longman, 1998.

MLA Handbook. 8th ed., MLA, 2016.

Njan Gandharva. Directed by Padmarajan. Goodnight Films,1991.

Sethuraman, V.S ."Indian Aesthetics: An Introduction".Macmillan India,1992.

Shakespeare, William. *A Midsummer Night's Dream,* edited. Robert Wilks. London. Machmillan Publishers, 1984.

Tumbhad. Directed by Rahi Anil Barve. Eros International, 2018.

CHAPTER V

PSYCHOTIC DISORDERS LEAD TO SAVAGERY

Ms. Charanprit Kaur
Asst.Teacher, St. Anthony's High School,
Mumbai, charanprit231@gmail.com

Abstract

The research paper incorporates an introduction of criminology psychology of a person mindset of a personality spirit of those who prone to some crime in life. Development of that character that shaped their life into imprisonment all their life. Their behaviour, incite action to their criminality. Gathering and scrutinizing the verifiable data are been discussed and the relationship between law and social sciences in the study of crimes is summarized. From the *Mindhunter* series, the diverse behavioural pattern is studied for their criminalised actions of murdering brutally and still accusing the corpse of the victim. Such cruelty has led them to shift to the dark hole which is infinite colossal in nature. Even *Lord of the flies* and Aileen's case have been included which states that rejection, abuse, torment, during preadolescence have been elucidated. Sociological theories are noteworthy, but not to the exclusion of the classical, positive, physiological, psychiatry and psychological theories. The horrifying childhood affairs have led some persons to take some harsh and cruel decisions so as to remove their frustrated mind on the dead corpse or an alive being.

Keywords: Embarrassment, Criminology, Rejection, Trauma and Cruelty.

• • •

"The chief problem is any community cursed with crime is not the punishment of the criminals, but the preventing of the young from being to crime" -W. E. B. Du Bois.

Psychotic Disorders Lead to Savagery

Criminal psychology is the study of the mindsets and nature of criminals. It answers the question: why do criminals do what they do? (What is Criminal Psychology? Exp 2 L 2 & 3) Psychology is the mindset nature of the person to engage with some criminalised mind. Never being realised that's a path of a misdemeanour. There's a satisfaction of hurting them or being judged by everyone. It's been shocking to realize that the misdemeanour one is who always engages with a camouflaged mindset.

Criminal activity is hideous for everybody. Never to be attained belief on the suspected of trusting of completing a certain task. Majorly the person needs psychological treatment. Due to the difference in the mindset of the treatment name, our people get tuned to an alright perspective. The idea of leading someone of some group dominates the nature of righteousness. The *Burari* family killing of 11 people of being surrounded with a spirited soul is present around one, who has affected the whole family by killing members of the family around. In the *Mindhunter* series, the content is focused on criminal psychology. Their pattern of behaviour, their mindset, the living nature of. In today's scenario mass killing has become so common, that every corner has incidents based on their mindset. The learning of the genetic causes of mental disorders includes both the laboratory analysis of the human genome and the statistical investigation of the recurrence of a specific disorder's episodes among individuals who share related genes i.e. the family inheritors. By the family histories, they compared the relevant frequencies in the ordinary instance of a mental illness in the close blood relations in the mainstream population. First-degree relatives (parents, siblings, and children) share 50 per cent of their genetic material with the patient, and higher rates of illness in these relatives than expected indicate a possible genetic factor.

Psychotic Behaviour due to Embarrassment of Society

In the case of Iran 2020, A daughter, Romina 14 years was beheaded with a farming sickle due to her love interest of her boyfriend of 29 years old by her father Reza Ashrafi. (A Daughter Is Beheaded, and Iran Asks if Women Have a Right to Safety Exp 2 L 17). The physical damage which is being involved with a victim and killer cause the traumatic effect of others too Freudian theory views childhood as the primary breeding ground of neurotic conflicts. It is due to children being fairly vulnerable and dependent on their parents for affection, care, emotional building and their psychosexual aggressive and impetuous decisions are not yet collaborated into an ordinary personality foundation. The theory propounded that children lack the resources to procure with emotional traumas, vulnerabilities and resentment, if these all develop into unresolved intrapsychic conflicts that the adolescent clench with abeyance through repression, there is an increased likelihood that insecurity, unease, or guilt will subtly influence the developing personality, thereby affecting the person's interests, attitudes, and ability to cope with later stresses.

The disorder leads to change in the path of disparaging behaviour of victimisers, their nature turns up to as suicidal, murderers, manipulators etc. If one enters into weirdos' ways, their change of mindset towards their life would be drastically changed. Holden the main protagonist of the *Mindhunter* series, carries out the different techniques of the criminal mind. He scientifically studies their insecurities, jealousy, fear, rejections in life, abuse, death by torcher, debased violence, mayhemthese all lead to the way of pleasure, or hap in the life of psychopaths. For instance, Ed Kemper would justify his criminal actions by stating meaningful to his mother towards men and him. The killing actions of self and others is a way of self-destructive.

These actions laid them down since their morale was down from their trusted ones. In Mindhunter, When Ed Kemper's actions were described as he prosecuted with hitting his mother on the head, by chopping off her head, intimating with the corpses relates to how he has been disregarded her mother in his life, though she has been at the honourable position in the administrative work. His mother's relation relative to his father was a major cause of crime. Both parents were disregarding their child and admonished him as a mental patient at a growing age. The fact of justifying their criminal act is somewhere empathetic but definitely couldn't equalize their mercy of being pardoned. The act of killing is promptly way, that how Ed Kemper was aggressive towards him and people he loved. (Season 1 Ep.2, 44:46-34:53, 31:19-27:02,17:14-12:20, Ep. 3 19:06-11:42)

Rejection, Isolation turns into Cruelty

In Brudos case, he presumed his criminal action was accepted under forceful actions of inspectors. The evidence that they received from his wife, was as such more of the feminine in approaching towards her. As the statement is being given that, stealing the lingerie of cloth lines, photographing the neighbourhood girl nakedly when he was fifteen age. Liking towards women's shoes were his prime interest. He got stilettos, which he used to pleasure himself. Holden learns from Brudos, others murderers' techniques to study their mindset of killing the woman who Brudos has photoshopped and later she was murdered. Brudos has confessed about trapping a girl in a tunnel at the age of 9 or 10, she was like the white shape in the darkness. He made her do things that she wasn't ready about. (MindhunterS.1 Ep.7 50:28-43:25, 35:45-27:29, Ep.8 39:17-32:17). As per the psychologist's approach, the errant and criminal nature by focusing on individual behaviour is based on the individual's personality. In specific, they concentrate more on nature or behaviour which has been restrained by them are learned. Among the earliest psychological theories of crime were those based on the work of Sigmund Freud, Freud argue that human nature includes a great reservoir of instinctual drives that demand gratification.

These propel are restricted by moral and ethical codes that children equate as a result of their great love and attachment to their parents. Adults develop their logical behaviour which liaises between their ego and superego. Because of their relatively restrained nature, criminality is assumed to result from the failure of their superego, a consequence of its incomplete development. Hence, the empirical nature of the evidence for this theory is thin. Later psychologists' theories of crimes were made on behaviour theory as that of B. F. Skinner, mentioned all human nature – criminal or otherwise – as learned and thus manipulated by the use of reinforcement and punishment. The social learning theory of Ronald Akers expanded behaviour theory to encompass ways in which behaviour is learned as compared to family members and intimate groups. In the 1990s, psychological research was taken out in which early childhood experiences including poor childhood experiences, poor-parental techniques, rejecting them as individuals, were learned which were later affected to the adult's life. Later, research also isolated impulsivity, engaging in immediate grief, easily distracted by the common remarks, which associates with criminality.

The case of Benjamin and Frank here is the criminals where Benjamin has a mental serious illness. The sociological theories say, the extending and influencing contact to the outside social group who commits crimes. Benjamin was the one who had the relationship with Beverly Jean. Beverly Jean was raped and killed, and a few days later her breast was cut off. These severities of crimes hold the weakness, rejection, boredom of the murderer. Her murder was not done by one, but by three people who came after supporting the murderer. (Season1, Ep. 6 19:00-16:48). These sociological theories assert that crime is the primary responsibility of a biologically and psychologically normal individual to social conditions that are abnormal and criminogenic. Edwin Sutherland put forwarded differential association theory, which argues that criminal behaviour is normal learned behaviour, that the learning takes place in a process of interpersonal communication with other people, that is consists primarily in the learning of ideas about whether laws are to be obeyed and the learning of criminal behaviours is determined primarily by the extent of the person's contact with other people who themselves engage in criminal activities.

A *Beautiful Mind* where the main protagonist is schizophrenic, but still he manages to get in the efforts of calculations, or to fit in the normal world. Lee Robins popularized the theory that offending is one element of a larger syndrome of anti-social behaviour, including heavy drinking, drug-taking, reckless driving, educational problems, employment problems, difficulties in relationships and so on. The is a primary antisocial personality disorder. Robins also argued that anti-social personality is obvious early in life and that it tends to persist from childhood to adulthood, with different behavioural manifestations. Mostly these types of people are naturally self-seeking pleasure, self-indulgent. Another typical conception is that people are motivated to maintain an optimal level, if their level falls below the optimum, they will try to rise it, whereas if it exceeds the optimal, they will strain to reduce it. A psychological theory often includes cognitive levels which say that the people choose to offend in a particular situation. Psychologists are committed to the scientific study of human behaviour with its emphasis that can be tested are falsified using empirical theories, quantitative data, controlled experiments, systematic observation, valid and reliable measures. Mostly various results predict poor parental behaviour or impulsiveness.

William Golding, *The Lord of the Flies* where children drop themselves on an island. To move from the island, they make the leaders lead the way for coming out of islands. They decide they light up the fire to give a signal for their existence on the island. Ralph and piggy have got the conch from the beach. That assembles the group for leading they're but there was one boy Jack who wanted to lead their group and turn them into a savage. Soon they start to believe there's a monster lurking around the forest that will eat all. So, they turn themselves into tribal ones and start hunting for the monster. They end up killing Simon with their bare hands and teeth. Simon had a horrible vision for the head is speaking, the *Lord of the flies*, he faints. After some time, he wakes up he had been to the mountain where he saw a dead parachute. He realizes soon, there is no monster around, its existence is there inside. There's the monster in every human being, it's our ways how we control and nurture it. Like this, many children turned savage and kill their friends instead of their monster character.

In *Mindhunter*, there's a criminal, Miller who acts psychotic at first by pointing out the gun to Ms Curtwell and making a demand to talk to his wife. He has been on some medications of mind, while he says he has been invisible for everyone. Until Holden acts to be preventive for him, to not cross the line of insanity he shoots himself. These have been the serious diagnosed psychotic nature, where one harms to others or himself as a suicidal note. Sigmund Freud stated that one can understand human behaviour best during childhood experiences. Criminal actions are linked to guilt feelings i.e. unsolved oedipal and Electra. As per to Freudian approach, John Bowlby studied that early maternal deprivation relates to delinquent behaviour (Season1, Ep.6 19:00-16:48).

Aileen Carol Wuornos originally her name was Aileen Pittman born Feb 29, 1956, in Florida. She is an American serial killer who murdered at least six to seven people in 1989-90. She had trouble childhood, her parents separated before her birth and her father spent time in mental hospitals for child molestations. She and her brother had been sent to live with her grandparents. Somewhere, her grandfather also kicked them out. She has been imprisoned for driving while intoxicating and for firing a gun from a moving vehicle. She has turned herself into a lesbian by nature. Her love Selby Wall was quite ignorant about her sentiments. To work her relationship up, she entered to prostitution for surviving. For survival, she has ended up in prostitution where she ended up killing men. In her defence, she has said that they were trying to end her life too by choking her up and through harmful vocals by those men. She has been punished with a death sentence with a lethal injection lately.

Throughout her life, whomever she had met, had rejected the way she was. Prostitution wasn't her cup of tea, but she had to choose it so that she can earn money and fill her stomach, Selby had shifted to her grandmother. She didn't have the courtesy to invite her up to her grandmother's house, instead, she started blaming Aileen, that she isn't worth anything because she doesn't have money. Somewhere Aileen wasn't accustomed to men around her, because she didn't like it simply. So, prostitution had deeply affected her to criminalize herself over everybody. She has been diagnosed with antisocial behaviour, which includes genetic factors such as abnormalities in the prefrontal cortex of the brain, including maternal drug use during pregnancy, birth complications, low birth weight, prenatal brain damage, traumatic head injury, and chronic illness. The psychoanalyst began to realize the woman may have dissociative symptoms related to a trauma she may have experienced as a child. Following through the work of the subconscious mind carried on by the psychoanalyst, she began to have hallucinations of being tied up to a chair and being abused.

The analysis regulated by Jung and Riklin is considered in the article on psychoanalysis, they found that the process of association is a process that is beyond subjects' control and awareness plays an essential role in the action of bondage. The analysis regulated by Jung and Riklin is considered in the article on psychoanalysis, they found that the process of association is a process that is beyond subjects' control and awareness plays an essential role in the action of bondage.

Conclusion

The above instances exemplify the mind's power to dissociate traumatic events and bury them into our unconscious memory because they are too painful. While rehashing these events was painful, the woman was able to work through the behaviours and emotions related to her trauma that she was playing out in other aspects of her life such as social and professional relationships. The vulnerability of a person has led the different ways in life negative or positive, it depends on the individual whether the life has to be turned into some reminiscing moments or whirl it around some drudgery chaos. The actions of all the imprisoned people have somewhere veered them into the easy task, which made them into criminals of brutality minds.

Works Cited

"Criminology: Intellectual History - Sociological Theories." *Sociological Theories - Criminal, People,*

Crime, and Theory - JRank Articles, law.jrank.org/pages/ 913/Criminology-Intellectual-History-Sociological- theories.html.

Drayton, Lindsey A. Drayton, et al. *Psychopaths Fail to Automatically Take the Perspective of Others.*27Mar.2018,

Golding, William. *Lord of the Flies.* Faber & Faber, 17 Sept. 1954. London, 1954.

Fassihi, Farnaz. "A Daughter Is Beheaded, and Iran Asks If Women Have a Right to Safety." *The New York Times*, The New York Times, 7 June 2020,

www.nytimes.com/2020/06/07/world/middleeast/honor-killing-Iran-women.html.

Lewis, Alexa, et al. "Introductory Psychology Blog (s14)_a." *Introductory Psychology Blog S14A*, 5 Feb. 2014.

sites.psu.edu/intropsychs14n1/tag/psychoanalysis/

"Major Concepts and Theories." *Encyclopædia Britannica*, Encyclopædia Britannica, Inc., www.britannica.com/science/criminology/Major-concepts-and-theories.

Mcleod, Saul. "Psychoanalysis." *Psychoanalysis | Simply Psychology*, 1 Jan. 1970.

www.simplypsychology.org/psychoanalysis.html.

Mindhunter. 16 Aug. 2019.

created by Asif Kapadia performance by Jonathan Groff, Holt McCallany, Anna Torv season1,episodes1- 10, Denver and Delilah Productions,2019.

satyavrat1994 Follow. "Unit 2 Criminal Behaviour Theories." *SlideShare*

www.slideshare.net/satyavrat1994/unit-2-criminal-behaviour-theories.

Schmideberg, Melitta. "Psychological Factors Underlying Criminal Behavior." *Journal of Criminal Law and Criminology (1931-1951)*, vol. 37, no. 6, 1947, p. 458., doi:10.2307/1138956.

Smith, Abbe. *The ÌMonsterî in All of Us: When Victims Become Perpetrators.* 3 Jan. 2005.

cpb-us-e1.wpmucdn.com/sites.suffolk.edu/dist/3/1172/files/2005/03/SmithFinal.pdf.

"Theories of Causation." *Encyclopædia Britannica,* Encyclopædia Britannica, Inc.

www.britannica.com/science/mental-disorder/ Theories-of-causation.

"What Is Criminal Psychology?" *Online Psychology Degrees,* 5 Feb. 2022.

https://www.online-psychology-degrees.org/study/ criminal-psychology/

YouTube, YouTube, 14 Dec. 2020.

https://www.youtube.com/watch?v=me0jsPJ2sWs.

Accessed 8 Feb. 2022.

Bio-Note

Ms. Charanprit Kaur presently works as a teacher, researcher. With a master's in English from the University of Mumbai, She successfully completed a certification course in Creative Writing from the esteemed St. Xavier's college and literature-based community platform Dark room poets. Her research interest area of interest revolves around Psychology, Cultural studies, literary theory, Media and communication, criminology and her current research revolve around Criminal Psychology, the rejections lead the way of the path of crimes, their intentions have been reviewed and scrutinized from the perspective of society in contemporary world literature.

CHAPTER VI

NARRATING FEMALE BILDUNG

Ms. Lalitha Sarma R.
Doctoral Research Scholar
Department of English
Sri Sathya Sai Institute of Higher Learning, Anantapur Campus

Abstract

Feminist studies aim at remodelling the desiderata of society by focusing on the inscription of the female subject in culture and exposing the ways in which the 'universal,' 'humanistic' principle is almost always contradicted both in terms of textual violation and sexual violence. The endeavour is at liberating women from those established structures and cultural constructs that persistently marginalise and inform the 'feminine.' The discovery, reconstruction and reconstitution of the idea of the female subject can be done only through a study of the deep-rooted leitmotifs and themes that manifest in literary works.

Narratives of the exploration of the feminine psyche – via resilience post-empowerment or regression – is crucial in that it helps unravel the recurrent patterns of this *Bildung* and ascertain if there be any universality in woman's experience, an interface sans cultural context, sans linguistic or regional divide or sans all shadow lines. It can help discover the *process* of gender difference and lead us to explore if gender is indeed a cultural construct. Understanding the cultural inheritance that operates in people's minds comprises 'myth'. The narrative traditions would thus be participative myths: myths that are not just stories of primordial, universal events; but rituals and events that are made and remade, enacted and distilled, in contemporary times, in an individual's mind. This paper aims at exploring how myths embedded in feminist narratives hold a crucial role in the study of the psychic development of the feminine and the feminine development of the psyche.

Keywords: Bildung, myth, difference and feminist psychoanalysis.

• • •

Narrating Female Bildung

All issues that fall within the portfolio of Gender Studies are reducible to the problem of *difference. The difference* appears as hierarchical binary opposition in dominant order and is structured in pairs of fundamental dualities such as mind and body, culture and nature, reason and imagination, man and woman. In the existing patriarchal system, structured on this binary thinking, the masculine constitutes the norm, the positive, whereas a woman is an aberration, the negative. She is defined in relation to what man is not, as "lack," of not being a man. Having no identity of her own, she often serves as an empty space, upon which he may project his desires within the stipulations of the existing and permitted system. In her oft-quoted words, Simone de Beauvoir pointed out the issue of how men see women as "the Other:" She is 'incidental, the inessential as opposed to the essential. He is the subject, he is the Absolute — she is the other' (Rajni Walia, 3).

The question of *difference* is not merely one of having a man as the referent or exploring how a woman is different from a man. It is also about seeing women as 'flat embodiments of a particular force or theme,' and 'mythically, allegorically, symbolically, but never realistically as fully rounded complex human beings,' (Rajni Walia, 3) i.e., the *difference* is also about how different women are from what men think they are. As Gayle Greene and Coppélia Kahn remark, in their essay "Feminist Scholarship and the Social Construction of Woman," more is involved than the bifurcated comprehension of experience:

the dichotomization of masculine and feminine in terms of such polarities as 'culture and nature, 'truth and duplicity', 'reason and passion', 'day and night' – the terms associated with the female always requiring control by the superior male. Thus the meaning of gender in patriarchal ideology is '*not* simply "difference", but...division, oppression, inequality, interiorized inferiority for women' (Barret 1980, pp 112-13) (Green and Kahn, 3-4).

Feminist studies aim at remodelling the desiderata of society. They focus on the inscription of the female subject in culture and expose the ways in which the 'universal,' 'humanistic' principle is almost always contradicted both in terms of textual violation and sexual violence. In its strategy of deconstructing the mechanisms of patriarchy in creating a cultural mindset, feminist literary studies set out on a two-pronged attack of the existing system that involved exposing the male versions of the world, and exploring the nature of the female outlook, as well as reconstructing the lost and suppressed records of feminine experience. The endeavour is to liberate women from those established structures and cultural constructs that persistently marginalise and inform the 'feminine.' The discovery, reconstruction and reconstitution of the idea of the female subject can be done only through a study of the deep-rooted leitmotifs and themes that manifest in literary works as a narrative strategy, various temporal and spatial metaphors, linguistic patterns and, most importantly, thematic design.

'Women Narratives of Self Empowerment is crucial because they depict the feminine *Bildung* or 'the internal life of female characters in the process of self-discovery' (Greene and Kahn, 48). Collating such sagas of feminine self-search would help us ascertain if there indeed is recurrent pattern or universality on woman's experience, an interface sans cultural context, sans linguistic or regional divide or sans all "shadow lines."

Psychoanalysis is a useful tool for feminists because of its psychological definition of gender. It makes diverse inroads in the efforts of feminist scholarship to challenge and change the tradition that has long silenced and marginalised women. It does so by deconstructing predominantly male paradigms and reconstructing a female perspective and experience. In feminist literary studies, psychoanalysis provides assistance by studying the psychodynamics of female characters and their authors, deriving the psychoanalytic patterns of textual metaphor, and eliciting patterns from the psychodynamics of gendered readings. It investigates the interaction of conscious and unconscious elements in the collective mind and gleans out the specific features of difference such as gender perspective and point of view, gender subjectivity in representations of displacement, and gender 'absence,' involving reading against the grain of the text. Feminist psychoanalytic criticism aims at discovering processes of gender difference. Critics have also observed that consciousness-raising in feminist groups is akin to the bringing up of the repressed into consciousness in therapy or the hoisting of the sub-text in literary criticism: all these are ways of learning about the previously unexpressed effects of patriarchy. In its functions as a political movement and as literary practice, feminism is analogous to psychoanalysis in the use of the model of repression. Woman's experience is often held as repressed or as embedded in the 'unconscious.' Diane Purkiss, in "Women's Rewriting of Myth," remarks:

Since Freud and Jung alike represented myths as part of the masculine cultural unconscious, femininity was constructed as the unconscious of the unconscious, the dark continent of the dark continent (Irigaray, 1985; Grosz, 1990). In psychoanalysis, a crucial notion is that the return of what has been repressed or silenced has the power to undo the stable constructions of identity and culture built on its repression (see Mitchell, 1974).... The return of the feminine has the power to shake male culture by undoing its central logic. (Larrington, 448)

An understanding of the cultural inheritance and the collective unconscious that operates in people's minds comprises 'myth.' 'Myth' is etymologically derived from the Greek word '*mythos*,' meaning word, speech, story, or legend. Myths are not just stories of primordial, universal events. They are made and remade, enacted and distilled, in contemporary times, in an individual's mind. Carolyne Larrington, states in the "Introduction" to *TheFeminist Companion to Mythology*:

Myth furnishes us with more than a repertoire of literary plots and themes, however. Mythology, the study of myth, introduces us to new ways of looking at social structures so that we can examine constants and variables in the organization of human society, in particular ...

women's role across different cultures and historical periods....

Within the study of mythology, female figures have too often been reviewed reductively, purely in terms of their sexual function and thus confined in a catch-all category labelled fertility....Women need to know the myths which have determined both how we see ourselves and how society regards us. (Larrington, ix)

Thus, myth is a key term in feminist discourse. Much of mythology passes down into the oral tradition. Whatever is handed down, from one generation to another, is preserved, but it still undergoes change. We see that, across cultures, myths lay great emphasis on feminine virtue, chastity and sacrifice. A clear dichotomy may be perceived in the inscription of the female subject in culture and myth. Alongside the celebration and portrayal of woman as a deity, and 'mother', she is also viewed as 'Kaanchan Kamini,' i.e., as one who functions as a seductive figure, arousing passion. This inherent contradiction is the finest instance of the unstable signification of woman that pervades the socio-cultural, mythic-poetic strata. In Indian spiritual parlance, a woman is revered as an embodiment of 'power', as a universal mother. But, she is also equated to death and feared as the ultimate pitfall in a pilgrim's progress. Though myths project women as powerful, they are always considered secondary. Women are presented in stereotyped, restricted roles. Psychoanalytic studies of women narratives unravel certain archetypes that recurrently appear in myths and legends. Myths embedded in feminist narratives hold a crucial role in the study of the psychic development of the feminine and the feminine development of the psyche.

Where Shall We Go This Summer? by Anita Desai is a powerful novel replete with inherent complexities and contradictions that give much scope for psychoanalytic study. The protagonist of the novel, Sita is in some sense a victim of psychological oppression. Unlike her mythical namesake, who refuses to reconcile with her husband after rejection when she is in the family way, Desai's pregnant-for-the-fifth-time Sita decides to go away from her husband Raman in order to confront herself. Whereas the Sita of Ramayana feels completely lost on her separation from her husband, but later grows into a woman character of great power when she refuses to undergo a second test to prove her chastity just to unite with her husband, Sita Desai's novel is almost a retraction of such feminist idealism. She undermines the glory associated with 'motherhood' by refusing to accept her biological role. The 'paranoiac show of rage, fear, and revolt,' (Desai, 20) 'the drama of her distress' (Desai, 23) results from the disillusionment of her faith in motherhood and nurturance. She comes to believe that 'The creative impulse had no chance, against the overpowering desire to destroy' (Desai, 30). Her horror is on account of the realisation that 'destruction came so naturally' (Desai, 30). She feels that -

By giving birth to the child now so safely contained, would she be performing an act of creation or, by releasing it in violent, pain-wracked blood-bath, would she only be destroying what was, at the moment, safely contained and perfect? More and more she lost all feminine, all maternal belief in childbirth, all faith in it, and began to fear it as yet one more act of violence and murder in a world that had more of them in it than she could take (Desai, 38).

Initially, she feels the need to move away from her husband and go to the haven of Manori. Unlike the ideal of liberated feminist heroines, Sita has no control over her reproductive abilities. Frustrated by her inability to cope with the pressures of her world, she hopes to run away from the terrifying ennui that defines her. But she realizes that she cannot keep the baby within her, but has to let it be born. The unborn baby represents the stereotype of a woman that society forces the woman to deliver when she is actually not so. She is unable to retain certain things that she does not wish to divulge. But since escapism is no truce with reality, latent must eventually surface. Under a destiny imposed upon her from outside for centuries together, women have reduced them to what they are.

A beautiful contrast to this helpless paranoid pregnant woman is Mrs. Vidya Bagchi, the protagonist of the 2012 Bollywood thriller, *Kahaani*. Subverting the protocols of male-dominated Indian filmdom, the movie is a rare original with no hero, no male-lead. The protagonist is a woman in the advanced stages of pregnancy in search of her missing husband who arrives at Kolkata, where she is a complete stranger. If pregnancy and womanhood were held hitherto as a symbol of creative flux and delicateness, the movie is a bombshell being a reversal of roles, subverting stereotypes and disrupting clichés. The symbolism of the movie is akin to the impact of Sylvia Plath's *Edge*. Two powerful women of the classical world are simultaneously evoked in Plath's *Edge*: the enrapturing and suicidal Cleopatra, and the murderous-mother Medea. Through her poetic gesture, Plath is asserting that femininity can be perfect or complete only in the freedom to both accept and refuse 'the organization of female sexuality under patriarchy, allowing women simultaneously to act out and refuse femininity' (Larrington, 454). The twin aspects which the woman contains, according to critics, is 'the female internalization of violence against women, and the female agent who externalizes that violence' (Larrington, 454). In *Edge*, Plath twines the two conflicting strands of thought as she 'identifies, rather than identifying with, a set of opposing stories about women's violence in relation to their bodies and their children.' (Larrington, 454) Purkiss pertinently remarks of Plath's poem and its motif of woman:

But she makes no gesture towards recuperating these stories for a socially sanctioned femininity. Rather the poem speaks from the position(s) of femininities driven out of society to be the violent other. More importantly, it refuses to take up a single position: the woman is not unequivocally either aggressor or victim, but neither and both. Plath speaks from the extreme and opposed positions they represent, the position designated as the limit, the absolute 'Edge.' The poem itself does a kind of violence to our ideas of what is appropriate, what can be said and who can say it. (Larrington, 454)

Likewise, Mrs. Bagchi's '*kahaani*' is a woman's journey to that absolute edge and subsequent entry into the interiors of the masculine hubris of society. It's a celebration of motherhood, though of a different kind: the festive air of Vijayadashami has a shade of sorrow: it miscarriage masquerading as pregnancy. In Vidya is embodied woman in totality: woman as the creator, protector and destroyer. Even the subtle suggestion of the tinge of romance between Satyoki "Rana" Sinha, the cop and the protagonist Vidya is an outstanding advancement of our collective perspective. Though initially, it is only a rural boy's fascination of London- returnee's computer skills, gradually this hero-worship becomes an adoration coupled with protective care. The concept of a bachelor falling in love with a pregnant woman is a very forward gesture in India, even on celluloid. In a society that shuns widows as inauspicious, Arup Basu's widow walks through the Durga Puja settings, vermillion smeared on her face, draped in a *lal paad* sari symbolising marriage and auspiciousness, having fulfilled her commitment to the deceased husband. The symbolism of Goddess Durga in slaying the evil is central to the film's tenor. The fake pregnancy and prosthetic abdomen, the 'truth' of her widowhood, her outstanding plot of making the IB a ploy in her act of vengeance all provide us with a novel and significant model of inverting the mythical construct of woman. The film reinstates the idea of Sri as Shakti; she is no more an abala. Self-empowerment and resilience acquire a different dimension in this context. Empowerment becomes self-discovery. Power in a woman is not a 'giveable' but a discoverable.

Conclusion

Among feminists, there is a strong emphasis on the 'constructedness' of universal femininity, and the influence of images and representations of femininity promulgated by literature, media and culture. The male point of view has long been accepted as the norm. Consequently, even women have come to internalise these culturally conditioned and received images of women. In order to escape typecasting in sexual identity, such conditioning has to be resisted. Gender roles must, therefore, be malleable and compliant, not inevitable and unchangeable givens. Mrs. Vidya Bagchi in Sujoy Ghosh's *Kahaani*, thus, is a powerful feminist hero who destabilises the fixities of gender, leading to fresh cultural representations. She is neither/ both the victim and the victimiser. The film is a visual and aesthetic metaphor. It is the narrative of a feminine Bildung, a woman's quest for meaning and fulfilment; but also it is Liebestod, a mystical moment of convergence of love and death. Just as blindness is the point of breakdown of painting as an art, the character of Mrs Vidya Bagchi deconstructs our stereotype of womanhood and motherhood.

Works Cited

Desai, Anita. Where Shall We Go This Summer? Delhi: Vihar Publishing House Pvt. Ltd., 1975.

Kahn, Gayke Greene and Coppelia, ed. Making a Difference: Feminist Literary Criticism. London: Routledge, 1985.

Larrington, Carolyne. The Feminist Companion to Mythology. London: Pandora Press, 1992.

Walia, Rajni. "Feminine self-appraisal in contemporary in contemporary women's fiction."

Women and Self: Fiction of Jean Rhys, Barbara Pym, Anita Brookner. New Delhi: Books

Plus, 2001. 1-4.

THE NEW GENERATION NATWARLAL'S OF CYBERSPACE

Asha P. Alias

Assistant Professor, Department Of Computer Science
Yeldo Mar Baselios College, Kothamangalam.

Abstract

In this modern world, cyber fraud is flourishing not only in India but across the world. So, it is very necessary to make ourselves aware of such cybercrimes. In most situations, the victims of cyber fraud are not the uneducated but the highly educated and well employed. When any such cybercrimes happen, many of the victims are not willing to complain because of their ignorance about the cyber laws. This article discusses the Pegasus Spyware and some common cybercrimes that are happening in day-to-day life, some ways to protect ourselves from being victims of such cybercrimes, and the cyber laws associated with it.

Keywords: Pegasus Spyware, Phishing, Cyber Extortion, Data Breach, Identity Theft and Harassment.

• • •

The New Generation Natwarlal's of Cyberspace

In the olden days, if we had to deal with only a few Natwarlal's, the digital revolution has made opportunities for several Natwarlal's to show their digital creativity in all wrong means. Almost everybody in this world is using the internet, smartphones or any other electronic device. According to the recent survey in the last six years that is from 2016 to 2021 cybercrimes too have risen throughout the country and was the highest during the covid 19 pandemic. But the amazing fact is that the detection rate is low. What does it mean? It is definitely because of our weak cyber security laws, lack of willingness to complain and unawareness.

Cyber Crimes – An Overview

Be it the olx or credit card scam, India is always at the receiving end of cyber security frauds. Recently leaked news on Pegasus spyware raises questions on our data security. The iPhone which is considered mostly secure was under the scanner following the Pegasus leaks. The cyber scam, as well as the fraud industry, is flourishing in India and across the globe.

Recently an online YouTube channel exposed a well-organized network operated from the national capital, looting the overseas victims by providing them virus removal services, which never exist. The scammers working under a fictitious BPO company will first inject a simple javascript full-screen popup through the browser with a message that the computer is under a virus attack and provide a toll-free number for the virus removal service. This all happens as if it's a proper Microsoft customer service centre number that the prospective victim has to call. The scam starts when someone calls their customer care and opts for the service. The scammers make the poor customers pay a hefty service charge for the virus removal, where they just disable the javascript script. In Fact, the victim can just restart the computer and in most cases, the script will be disabled. Thanks to the ethical hacker from the US the complete gang is under police custody. Our weak cyber security laws or implementation paves the way for these scammers to flourish.

If the above incident only targets the people using smart devices or laptops, what is more, alarming is the fact that even someone who has a basic phone and a debit card can be easily scammed. Recently my brother who is residing in Bangalore went to their nearby panipuri stall where an uneducated North Indian guy sells pani puri for his livelihood. As my brother was a regular customer there, that guy showed him some messages which he got from his bank. When he went through the messages he got to know that guy has been scammed for ?50000. My brother advised him to immediately contact the bank but in most cases, the customers are not going to get their money back. I was totally puzzled how this scam happened when the person is not even using a smartphone. Later when I discussed it with one of my cybersecurity friends, I got to know about a new scam. The scammers will link the UPI id of the victim on their phone and transact on their behalf. The biggest mistake the poor chap has made was to share his OTP and card number.

In the above two incidents, if the victims were not quite educated and were unaware of the consequences of sharing the OTP, there are cases where the scammers have tricked even the well-educated ones. The interesting factor here is most of the scammers are school dropouts and come from a very poor backgrounds. In fact, most of them don't even think of it as a crime.

Major cyber crimes across the world

India is not the only country that is attacked by cybercriminals but the whole world. As the world is moving towards the digital revolution, these activities are going to increase in many folds. The government and the common citizens should work hand in hand to tackle cybercriminals. Some of the major modus operandi used by cybercriminals are as follows:

1. Phishing

I am sure that many of us would have received e-mails or messages over Whatsapp or social media, with a link to earn rewards as part of Amazon or Flipkart anniversary celebrations. Many of us would have even clicked on that link without even knowing that it's a fake one and could be a phishing attempt. Phishing is a type of cybercrime that is used to steal confidential data like passwords, credit card details etc. On clicking the link we would be directed to a fake login page that resembles an original one. Once we submit the login credentials and click on the login button, the attacker will receive our credentials and can misuse them. Fortunately, phishing can be easily avoided by being a bit careful with the email attachments and links:-

Never open a spam email.

Always look at the link if it's a genuine one (for example amazon. in not amazon.in)

Always use a trusted antivirus solution on your devices.

2. Cyber Extortion

This is comparatively a new way of cybercrime. Recently many people are getting video calls on their WhatsApp from unknown numbers and once the receiver attends the call, he will be shown some obscene self videos of the calling party. Now even if we disconnect the call the calling party would have recorded our video and can extort money by threatening to leak it over social media. Many times these criminals succeed in extorting the money. If we have been a victim of these attacks, the first thing is not to worry as we haven't done anything wrong and immediately complain to the cyber crimes department of our respective state. Under no circumstance, we should pay them the money. With the advancement of technology, criminals can be easily tracked.

3. Data Breach

Recently there was a major outcry in India following the pegasus row. Many of the political leaders and personalities were allegedly spied on through spy software installed on their phones by an Israeli company. Even the iPhones, which were known for their privacy were not spared. The worrying fact here is that unlike phishing the spying software was installed in the phone through a WhatsApp missed call. The government should come up with strict data privacy guidelines like the GDPR laws in Europe or CCPA of the US where the law breaching companies have to pay a hefty penalty. We also have data privacy laws in India but the government has to focus on strengthening the same.

4. Identity theft

Identity theft is another major type of cyber attack. We hear daily news where the victim shares their bank OTP and loses the money to the cyber frauds. One of the major incidents of Identity thefts and fraud happened in Bangladesh in February 2016, when a hackers group from North Korea entered into the Bangladesh Central Banks high-security systems through a hacked employee system. The bank lost US$951 million through a fraudulent international wire transfer. Investigators found malware attacks on the bank network system which could be because of the outdated operating system and security software.

5. Harassment

Another main cybercrime is where the criminals use morphed photographs of the victims and post it over social media to malign the victims. We should be careful while posting our personal photographs or information on public forums. We should always lock our profiles to unknown persons.

Cyber Laws of India.

As the internet grows so do cybercriminals. Sometimes even after being cautious we may fall on these traps and may need protection from the law. Cyber Laws in India("IT Act 2000") came into force on October 17, 2000. It contains 94 sections which are divided into 13 chapters and 4 Schedules. The main purpose of the Act is to provide legal recognition to electronic commerce and to facilitate the filing of electronic records with the Government.

Section 65 – Tampering with Computer Source documents

If a person wittingly or advisedly conceals, destroys or alters or advisedly or wittingly causes another to cover, destroy or alter any computer ASCII file used for a pc, program, automatic data processing system or electronic network, once the pc ASCII file is required to be unbroken or maintained by law. Penalty - Imprisonment up to a few years, or/and with fine up to two lakh rupees.

Section 66 – Hacking with computer system

if a person with the intent to cause or knowing that he's doubtless to cause wrongful loss or harm to the public or someone destroys or deletes or alters any data.

Penalty - Imprisonment up to a few years, or/and with fine up to 500,000Rs.

Section 66B - Accepting stolen computer or electronic devices

A person receives or retains a pc resource or communication device that's understood to be purloined or the person has reason to believe is purloined.

Penalty - Imprisonment up to 3 years, or/and with fine up to RS 100,000.

Section 66C – Using password of another person

A person fraudulently uses the key, digital signature or alternative distinctive identification of another person.

Penalty - Imprisonment up to 3 years, or/and with fine up to RS 100,000.

Section 66D – Cheating using computer resource

If a person cheats somebody employing a pc resource or communication.

Penalty - Imprisonment up to a few years, or/and with fine up to RS 100,000

Section 66E – Publishing private images of others

If anyone captures, transmits or publishes pictures of a person's private parts while not his/her consent.

Penalty - Imprisonment up to 3 years, or/and with fine up to RS 200,000

Section 66F – Act of cyber terrorism

If anyone denies access to licensed personnel to a pc resource, accesses a protected system or introduces material into a system, with the intention of threatening the unity, integrity, sovereignty or security of our country, then he commits cyber terrorism

Penalty - Imprisonment up to life.

Section 67 – Publishes obscene information in e-form

If anybody publishes or transmits or causes to be printed within the electronic type, any material that is sexy or appeals to the sexy interest or if its impact is like to tend to debauch and corrupt persons who are doubtless, having relevance all relevant circumstances, to read, see or hear the matter contained or embodied in it.

Penalty - Imprisonment up to 5 years, or/and with fine up to RS 1,000,000

Section 67A - Publishing images containing sexual acts

If anyone publishes or transmits pictures containing a sexual specific act or conduct.

Penalty- Imprisonment up to 7 years, or/and with fine up to RS 1,000,000

Section 67B – Spreading child pornography

If anyone captures, publishes or transmits pictures of a child in a very sexually specific act or conduct. If an individual induces a child into a sexual act. a child is considered as anyone beneath eighteen.

Penalty- 5 years of imprisonment, or/and with fine up to RS 1,000,000 on first conviction. 7 years of imprisonment, or/and with fine up to RS 1,000,000 on second conviction.

Section 67C - Failure to keep up records

Persons deemed as negotiant (such as AN ISP) should maintain needed records for a stipulated time. Failure is an offence.

Penalty- Imprisonment up to a few years, or/and with fine.

Section 68 - Failure/refusal to fits orders

The Controller may direct a certifying authority or any employee of such authority to cease performing such activities in accordance with the order if those are necessary to confirm compliance with the provisions of this Act, rules or any rules created there beneath. someone who fails to befits any such order shall be guilty of an offence.

Penalty- 3 years of imprisonment, and a fine of up to two lakh rupees

Section 69 - Failure/refusal to decrypt data

If the controller is pleased to know that it is necessary to take over and act in accordance with the interests of India's Sovereignty or integrity, state protection, friendly relations with the foreign countries or public order or prevention of any commissioning, the offence must be documented in writing by direct order to any agency The subscriber or someone answerable of the computer resource shall, once referred to as upon by any agency that has been directed, should extend all facilities and technical help to decode the knowledge. The subscriber or someone who fails to help the agency referred is deemed to own committed a criminal offense.

Penalty- Imprisonment up to 3 years, or/and with fine up to RS 200,000

Section 70 – Ensures access to a protected system

Any computer system or network is a protected system that is declared by the appropriate Government by notification within the Official Gazette, the suitable Government might, by order in writing, authorize the persons who are licensed to access protected systems. If an individual secures access or tries to secure access to a protected system, then he's committing an offence.

penality:10 years of imprisonment and a fine.

Section 71 – Misrepresentation

If anyone makes any falsity to or suppresses any material reality from, the Controller or the Certifying Authority for getting any license or Digital Signature Certificate.

Penalty - Imprisonment up to a few years and a fine of up to one lakh rupees.

Protective Measures

- Always use the updated software.

- Never click on unverified links.
- Never share the credentials like the OTP number, password etc.
- Never ever attend the videocalls from an unknown number.
- Never open the attachments or mails from untrusted sources.
- Always use antivirus software
- Use strong passwords so that nobody can guess your password.(Avoid setting mobile number, date of birth, house name as password)
- If any cyber crime happens immediately contact the cyber cell or call a nearby police station.

Conclusion

Cybercrimes are increasing day by day. Even if you have been learning computers since a young age, it is very necessary to include in the syllabus regarding cybercrimes and cyber laws. Today's children are tomorrow's citizens. By creating awareness about cyber laws and cybercrimes from an early age we can reduce cybercrimes to a certain extent. Once a cybercrime has taken place, it should be said out loud but many should not say it out of shame. This can again be prevented by filing a complaint in the cyber cell and catching and punishing the cyber thieves. Everyone should have the awareness that no one will ever give them money for free. If people listen to these things, we can get rid of Cybercrimes.

Works Cited

https://www.infosecawareness.in/cyber-laws-of-india
https://www.legalserviceindia.com/
https://en.wikipedia.org/wiki/Cybercrimes

TAKING A SECOND LOOK AT THE LENSES: DECONSTRUCTING FANTASISED WOMANHOOD IN MALAYALAM CINEMA

Treesa Petreena

Ph. D. Research Scholar

St. Xavier's College for Women, Aluva.

Abstract

Kerala society is appropriated by patriarchy, where gender hierarchies are highly nurtured. Women who are 'represented by men' are considered to be a part of this patriarchal circle, and thus 'real women' are seen as outcasts. A woman's body becomes a social and cultural construct while men enjoy a sense of toxic privilege in our society. Here, it is in this context that the role of cinema calls much attention as it acts as a watchdog and propagator of patriarchal ideologies. While analysing the history of cinema, only men had the access to power, opportunity and material resources as filmmakers, cinematographers and producers. Men controlled the scene not only as makers, but also as the majority of the spectators, and therefore male fantasies are exalted since cinema is 'made by men and for men'.

This research paper aims to re-read various instances and tropes within Malayalam Cinema and how it has aided in creating conditioned images of womanhood according to male fantasies. Also, the study intends to prove that the status of women remains unexplored and unknown unless it is narrated by female voices.

Keywords: Male gaze, abjection, cultural hybrid, voyeurism, hyper-realism, gender performativity, gender, absence and presence.

• • •

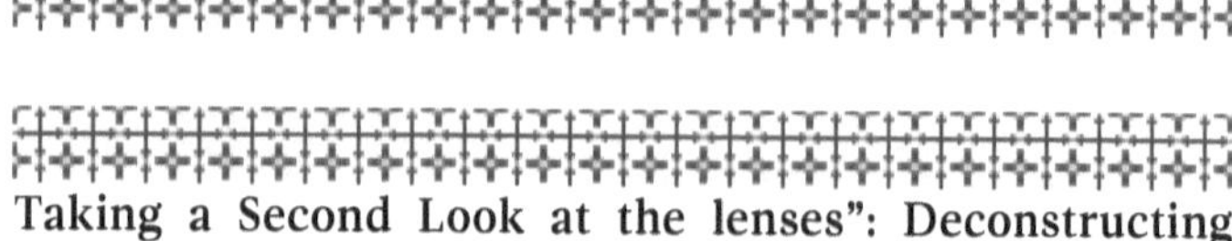

Taking a Second Look at the lenses": Deconstructing Fantasised Womanhoodin Malayalam Cinema

Among the Indian states, Kerala stands apart socially, culturally and politically in terms of high literacy rates, economic development, balanced sex ratio and lower infant mortality rates. Therefore, an illusion about women of Kerala enjoying greater empowerment circulates widely. But the fact is that, compared to women who enjoyed matrilineal advantages in certain communities in pre-independent Kerala, the modern women is in a double trap within the label of empowerment. Even though we have women's collective groups which advocate gender equality and workplace impartiality, it fails to address women's submissive position in family and relationships. The ironic situation of 'liberal patriarchal pseudo feminism that exists in Kerala continues to emphasise that women are essentially wives and mothers' (Pillai, 5). The prevailing state of our society puts the position of women problematic as well as confusing, that whatever their career designation may be, women hurries to get back to their households to settle down with their essential selves. Such forced notions of femininity which is regarded as normative eventually curtail a woman her actual identity.

The concept of 'modern womanhood' is materialised into reality when a woman steps out of her house. Our society never tolerated a progressive femininity within one's household, and was seen as a potential threat which could harm tradition and identity. The concept becomes acceptable only if the woman could balance domestic life with her radical outlook even-though it is self-contradictory. The myth of modern womanhood is thus "a mix of the dominant Victorian and brahminical values", and this idea was clearly reflected in cinemas (Virdi 62). Thus modern Kerala woman is a typical example of how one could never equalise a woman's higher literacy rates and salary scale with that of her liberation and independence. It was eventually a combination of a much stronger restraint that put together the upper-caste Hindu ideal and purity of Victorian remains, resulting in the formation of a new cultural hybrid.

For a deliberate erasure of the possibilities in modifying the oppressive means of patriarchy, the medium of cinema has been used to naturalise the essentialist notions of hegemonic culture. The unwritten but strictly nurtured protocols regarding gender expressions, sexuality and gender roles are widely circulated among the common mass by means of cinema. Cinema is a popular medium in which dominant cultural values are constantly contested through the construction of powerful images and through cinematic codes, gender roles are specifically assigned to each mainstream genders respectively. The formula for an ideal Indian woman or a man is the appropriate mixture of certain particular characteristic features like "submissiveness, self-sacrifice, traditional values, norms and attire, chaste, and virtues are feminine traits. Where on the other hand, dominance, rational, masculine and muscular bodies, protector, fearless, assertive and independent are all associated with masculinity and the heroes of the film"(Raza, 63).

Any departure from this agreement causes a rupture in the stability of the gender hierarchy and this is why the image of a 'social butterfly', that is "a metaphor for women of leisure" (Diwakar, 247), is always a problematic model, which is constantly ridiculed and shamed over the decades through the medium of cinema. A butterfly image is given for an educated and free-willed woman because "the metaphor evokes images of restless, flighty, colourful creatures who are difficult to pin down or control" (Diwakar, 248). In Malayalam cinema, such wild and independent image of a modern woman is highly at risk, which is always in comparison with the obedient and dutiful image of a traditional Indian woman who eventually wins the contest. Popular cinemas celebrate this notion of the 'heroine and the vamp' dichotomy, idealising the virtuous woman and comparing her to the Hindu mythological figures such as 'Sita'. The 'reckless' woman is taught a lesson by dragging her towards the limits of patriarchy, and is transformed to a traditional submissive woman, which she eventually learns as ideal and meaningful, as in the film *Aaramthampuran* (1997, directed by Shaji Kailas). Ambition is often seen as detrimental, and the women in male fantasy learn to give up on themselves.

The hatred towards modern femininity and the admiration for the traditional chaste innocent woman continues throughout Malayalam film history and in most of these films the problem is resolved, as the 'free-willed' woman submits herself by glorifying existing patriarchal norms. Most of the examples can be drawn from films of the 1990s such as *Njangal Santhushtaraanu* (1999),

Kaliveedu (1996), *Deepasthambham Mahashcharyam* (1999) etc. This modern to traditional transformation theme is repeated numerous times in Malayalam cinema and most of them are huge successes, which show how much the theme is desired and accepted by the audience. A similar threat posed through cinema is the village belle's desire towards urban ways, which is considered as a destructive cause of any ideal family. Number of films has been released on such theme, which proves that it has been always a dreadful nightmare for the patrilineal society. Films such as *Amma Ammayiamma* (1998), *Thalyana Manthram* (1990), *Ayalathe Adheham* (1992), *Sreekrishnapurathe Nakshathrathilakkam* (1998) etc. instruct women about the evilness of urban society and the sanctity of cosy family life in a village. The repeated assertions of these fabricated gender role performances through cinema, naturalises the phenomenon as essential and it is passed on to the succeeding generations.

Another ploy that is very frequently observed in movies is the veneration of 'motherhood' as an embodiment of kindness and self-sacrifice. The mother-son relation is often regarded as the personification of the relationship between the nation and its citizen, where the son is even willing to die for his mother's love. Here, the notion of motherhood is unnecessarily exalted and never portrays her as an ordinary human being with self-love. Kaviyoor Ponnamma is often casted as the ideal mother and through such characters only one ideal face of motherhood is shown and admired. Any mother who deviates from the ideal figure is pushed towards guilt and shame. The role of cinema cannot be undermined here as mere entertainment, but it is to be analysed with a critical eye as its reach is far and deep.

For several decades, the exclusion and silencing of women had been a common practice in the male-centred domain of cinema. Theories like Laura Mulvey's 'male gaze' and the feminist interpretation of Derrida's theory of 'Absence and Presence' in the context of cinema, have aided in widening an awareness about the objectification as well as passivity of women characters in film industry. The camera movements are directed in such a way as to interpret a woman's position agreeing to a man's fantasies, and only certain kind of women characters either 'black or white' are projected through films whereas the rest of the 'shades of grey', pertaining to the infinite dimensions of a woman's personality, are conveniently made invisible from the limelight as if they never existed. The Malayalam film industry is never distant from this reality of cementing the patriarchal propaganda through movies, where it acts as a watchdog of society.

While analysing the history of cinema, only men had the access to power, opportunity and material resources as filmmakers, cinematographers and producers. Men controlled the scene not only as makers, but also as the majority of the spectators, and therefore male fantasies are exalted since cinema is 'made by men and for men'. The foundation of male fantasies can be traced right back from the concept of the chivalric prince-charming coming in rescue of the beautiful and lost princess, and the variations of this concept are still circulated through our films. If Tamil and Hindi cinema portrays this fancied image directly in their films, Malayalam cinema, which is reputed for its realistic content, is adamant about keeping even that fantasy close to reality, which makes it even more frightening.

One of the many fantasies of man which recurs in Malayalam movies is that it is better to love or marry a beautiful innocent and ignorant woman rather than a bold, informed and career-oriented one who raises her opinions. The moral, financial and physical dependency of woman is much desired and appreciated by men in our society. *Narasimham* (2000), *Iniyum Kadha thudarum* (1985) *Vatsalyam* (1993) *Thooval Kottaram* (1996) etc are some of the examples that resonates patriarchy's inherent hatred toward bold women and obsession with innocence. The recurring image of 'Husband is God' trope seen in most of the Malayalam movies (eg: Balachandra Menon movies) is also a potential threat that encourages domestic violence, where wife is regarded as a slave. The opposite image where the wife becomes the decision-maker of a family (like in *Gandhi Nagar Second Street* (1986)) is usually inserted in a film as a laughter element and is portrayed with contempt and labels such men who cannot 'control' their wives as effeminate. Such naturalisation of gender performances make deep marks within the mind-set of audience and results in the realisation of such wronged ideologies.

A physical attack or misbehaviour is picturised as a romantic gesture in our films as in the movie *Kanmadham* (1998). The consent of a woman is given zero value and stalking her even after she says no to a marriage proposal is a common and accepted act in our movies. Stalking women and troubling her unless she says 'yes' is the theme of most of the songs produced in our film industry. The meaning of 'no' twisted and interpreted as 'yes' is definitely not an innocent act and circulation of such messages are quite distressing. Another demeaning act that is advocated in movies is the casual representation of sexual attacks against women and blaming the victim for the violence that occurred. Such culture treats a rape victim as an outcast and resolves the problem by making her marry the tormentor (Hitler, 1996). Rape is also seen as a way to teach free-spirited women a lesson. During the formative years of children, as they confront such negative awareness about gender performativity, sexuality, and gender binaries, the concept imbibed by them is quite precarious which lasts for a life time.

Gender parodying through cross-dressing is included in films to bring comic relief, and for the purpose usually male to female cross dressing is preferred in movies as it elicit much laughter and ridicule. *Mayamohini* (2012) is an apt example of gender parodying which flaunts male fantasy in the most offensive way. In the same manner through the film *Chandupottu* (2005) the transgender community has also been ridiculed and misinterpreted rudely and inappropriately sending wrong information about them, by which they suffered mercilessly before the public.

The happy and wealthy joint family trope is a very common image loaded with many misogynistic elements weaved into it. *Vazhunnor (1999)* is one among such many films which drew a clear cut definition for how men and women should act in a family and society. Here hero is a brave man from upper class family who resolves problem that concerns family honour and fulfils hyper- realism. All the men in the family are shown drinking and discussing their next fight with the villain, whereas women are always in the kitchen preparing meals. The family's meeting place is usually the dining room where women are seen to be serving men food and advising them not to go for further fights and retires to the kitchen itself. Here the women dwell mostly in the kitchen and they are seen in the lounge area for the purpose of serving tea for the male members.

The recent film *The Great Indian Kitchen* (2021) particularly satirises and critiques such acts of space occupation entitled to each gender types.

Jyothika Virdi in her work *The Cinematic imagination: Indian Popular Films as Social History* observes that "Reading women's lives from the film texts alone would be flawed, particularly when the lives of actual women, especially in the film industry, are an apogee to their screen representation (61). Women's direct experiences and fantasies hardly get recorded and the gap is obvious in the ratio between male and female-centric films that get released. Even though changes do occur in the current decade, where few female actors like Nayanthara and Manju Warrier emerge as female superstars amidst the chaos that happens in the film industry, it is impossible to avoid the fact that "women are still doubly vitiated and subordinated by a nationalist patriarchy and a sexist film industry" (61).

Man's position in our society is specially enriched with a kind of 'toxic privilege' where most of the societal institutions are developed in such a way as to nurture it even more, and cultural tools such as mass media, television and cinemas reflect it, so as to normalise such a privilege. In popular Indian films, men are represented as the bearer of power, meaning and strength who fights evil and resolves the problems. Here, male fantasies and perspectives are exalted since cinema is made by men and for men. When people constantly and repeatedly watch films from a male point of view, it moulds their thought process so as to neutralise male gaze and normalise it. Margaret Atwood in her work Robber Bride asserts about an ironic tendency - "You are a woman with a man inside watching a woman. You are your own voyeur". This is much applicable our society where women also becomes the proud spokesperson of patriarchy and male fantasies unknowingly.

The recent changes in the representation of women which tries to address real femininity in Malayalam cinema itself are proof of this positive evolution. Films like *22 Female Kottayam* (2012), *Rani Padmini* (2015), *Oru Muthassi Gadha* (2016), *Mayanadhi* (2017), *Ishq* (2019), *Jallikattu* (2019) are some of the notable films which have marked the beginning of an era that courageously portray the essence of real womanhood in Malayalam film industry. But unfortunately, there are not many women-centric movies narrated by female directors in Malayalam and a change is complete only when one's story is narrated by oneself.

There is an assumption that men are like open books, and women are complicated beings who are unable to decode. It is largely due to the fact that, almost all the dimensions of male characteristics and fantasies are explored through our films, while the existence of female fantasies remains unknown. A person or a community becomes ambiguous in their representation before the world when they remain unexplored. People, who are privileged and mainstream, develop discourses about the unknown, and usually end up misrepresenting them since their knowledge is incomplete. The perception of the West about the orient as 'exotic' as well as 'mysterious' is one such instance traced back from history and it proves that this pattern always recurs. Whenever the marginalised community fight back by telling stories from their perspective, a progressive change in their status is visible, making them less unknown and more acceptable. Overcoming this danger through the process of 'unlearning' is possible when more women get access to power in the film industry and receive the opportunity to material resources as filmmakers, cinematographers and producers.

Work Cited

Diwakar, Vaishali."Re-imagining Nation and redefining regional and gender identities in

the cinema of the 1950s". *Thinking Gender Doing Gender: Feminist Scholarship And Practice Today*, edited by Uma Chakravarthy, Orient Blackswan, 2018, 233-255.

Pillai, Meena T. *Women in Malayalam Cinema: Naturalising Gender Hierarchies.*

Orient Blackswan, 2010

" The problem with the "Male Gaze" in Hollywood." *Youtube*, uploaded by Brut America,

20 February 2021, https://youtube.be/1n3eS9ZLwWI. Accessed 01 March 2021.

Virdi, J. (2003), *The Cinematic ImagiNation: Indian Popular Films as Social History.*

Rutgers University Press, 2003.

Work Cited

Diwakar, Vaishali."Re-imagining Nation and redefining regional and gender identities in

the cinema of the 1950s". *Thinking Gender Doing Gender: Feminist Scholarship And Practice Today*, edited by Uma Chakravarthy, Orient Blackswan, 2018, 233-255.

Pillai, Meena T. *Women in Malayalam Cinema: Naturalising Gender Hierarchies.*

Orient Blackswan, 2010

" The problem with the "Male Gaze" in Hollywood." *Youtube*, uploaded by Brut America,

20 February 2021, https://youtube.be/1n3eS9ZLwWI. Accessed 01 March 2021.

Virdi, J. (2003), *The Cinematic ImagiNation: Indian Popular Films as Social History.*
Rutgers University Press, 2003.

CHAPTER IX

UNDERSTANDING TRANSGENDER STUDENTS: GENDER–INCLUSIVE EDUCATION IN B.ED. CURRICULUM

Archa Gopan

B.Ed. Student, KTCT College of Teacher Education
Kaduvayil, Thiruvananthapuram.

ABSTRACT

Understanding the transgender students and accepting them the way they are is the greatest help that the whole of society can do for them. Education can play a great role and so do the education systems. We are still in the traditional confinements that all students come to school with a gender identity that aligns with their biological sex and such is the way the curricula too are getting constructed. It is very much important to keep in mind that most students realize their gender identity during adolescence and that they experience a lot of pressure both from within and outside. Gender inclusion is a concept that speaks out the fact that male and female stereotypes do not define societal roles and expectations and there should not be any discrimination based on all these false notions. Gender inclusivity is to be incorporated into the field of education so that the students at a very young age will become socially aware of their own identities. As future teachers, the teacher trainees should be given proper awareness on how to help the students to get out of all sorts of conflicts and for which the curricula have to be updated.

Keywords: Transgender, B.Ed. Curriculum, Gender Inclusivity, Teacher Training.

INTRODUCTION

The world today is in a random pace of change; accepting and assimilating those changes need conscious effort. The paper is all about the need for bringing about such a progressive change in the curricular structure of education. The paper just talks about the advancements that B.Ed. the curriculum should welcome this era of varying perspectives. As we all know that teachers are of course in a way the light-bearers and problem solvers of many kids even in the era of online education, they have a great impact in shaping the personality and affecting the overall development of the children. So, it is the need of the hour that they have to be equipped with all sorts of skills to cater to the internal and external conflicts that these kids face.

Bachelor of Education is a course that aims at creating highly competent teachers. The curriculum of the course is designed in such a way that a person who enrols on this course will come out with all the effective strategies to cope up with the psychological problems faced by the students. As the course mainly aims at training the teachers for secondary school education, it is when the children go through the most complex phase of their life – adolescence. As Stanley Hall has rightly noted, "adolescence is a period of great stress and strain, storm and strife." It is the time when children get to know more about their bodies and thus encounter a lot of conflicts. Teachers can help them to overcome all these barriers that stand as a hindrance to their journey to the future. The teaching curriculum encompasses the psychology on how to deal with boys and girls, regarding their mental, emotional, physical, social and all such developments.

Transgender is an umbrella term that refers to a spectrum of persons whose gender expression is different from that of the assigned sex at birth. To keep the term pertinent to schools and colleges, we should be mindful of the fact that transgender students are those who self-identify and perceive themselves to be a gender that does not align with their natal sex. They always wanted to assert their identity in front of others and urge for acceptance. Teachers should be aware of the biological as well as the psychological traumas and conflicts that are associated with these students and they have to be treated without any discrimination like all other children. For this, teachers have to be made aware of how gender inclusivity can be made real in the school atmosphere.

UNDERSTANDING TRANSGENDER STUDENTS

A school is a place where each and every student who comes to seek knowledge should be treated with equality and dignity. The teachers are a set of guiding personalities who should be able to understand the students in each and every step in the process of growth and development. They always address to a group, the student community who are unique in their own ways. The ones who address the adolescent children need more experience as they are energetic and fragile at the same time.

Adolescence is a time when children undergo a lot of changes. It is the time when they grab a more authentic and clear idea about their own identity and sexual orientation. Students who cannot adjust to their natal sex feels a lot of pressure and they feel out of place due to gender non-conformity. They feel as if they belong to a body that they could not really adjust with. They try to call out to the whole society about who they really are and this stage of transition is not very easy to be handled and get handled and thus need proper guidance and support. Teachers should be able to identify such students who really need care, acceptance and proper care. As teachers, they should tell their students what they are going through or what their friends are going through and should find out the appropriate and the most effective ways to get away from their problems.

Acceptance from teachers and the whole group of administrators are highly significant in determining the mental and emotional state of transgender students. They do not have any mental anomalies and are not confounded by gender identity. They are only discontented and anxious over their natural sex. Transgender students should be provided with equal opportunities as that of others and they need constant representation in the field of education so that the social and cultural stigmas pertaining to their identities can be distanced apart from their lives. Advancement in the curriculum of teacher trainees with all these improvements can surely transform the mainstream perceptions of gender and its implications. The socio-economic situation of the transgender people in our country clearly indicates that education is out of reach for them. Their major concern is survival.

Every person is unique and no one behaves the same as others. Transgender students too vary in how they present themselves at school. Some of them may show gender non-conforming behaviour and some others may hide their gender identity as they fear harassment and neglect from family and society. The range of problems are so diverse and the teachers have to be aware of all these situations no matter how complex it is. There are some other students who decide to have gender transition while at school itself which requires more attention and care from the part of teachers. Some children find it very difficult to come out of the confinements of the traditional beliefs and family set up and they will suffocate for not being able to express their gender identity. Children are diverse and so do their problems. The ways to tackle these problems require different approaches and offering solutions to all these problems is not very easy.

Whenever a student intends to undergo gender transition while in their school, teachers along with the whole administrative system should provide a safer and more supportive environment. The process will have a greater impact on the student as it results in both physical, mental and emotional change, which is most often visible and vivid. Teachers should be very much equipped to clarify the doubts and conflicts of the whole classroom and thereby widening their thinking perspectives. It is through teachers that the students get an overall outlook about the world around them.

Addressing the issues and identity crisis of transgender students have become the need of the hour now. The social stigmas associated with them should be eradicated from society which could be done effectively through education. Education is a powerful tool that could bring forth drastic changes through the most powerful media - teachers and students. It is very much essential to make schools and colleges trans-friendly. They should never feel that they are different from others. They should be treated with all due respect and dignity that every other student in a school enjoys. We should strive to develop a society where this topic should become an invalid and outdated one to have a discussion.

GENDER INCLUSIVE EDUCATION IN B.Ed. CURRICULUM

Gender inclusion is a concept that transcends the notion of equality. Being the products of society, teachers most often might carry with them certain sorts of gender norms and so as to create a gender-inclusive classroom, the stakeholders of education have to be trained properly and should be imparted with the right kind of attitude and perspectives towards what in fact gender inclusivity is. Teachers should be more sensitive to the gender that is being presented in their classrooms. By reflecting on their own experiences on how gender is being shaped and demonstrated in our society, they are in fact shifting the culture to be safer and inclusive.

B.Ed. the curriculum mainly aims at training an ordinary person to be a highly competent teacher in such a way that they can cope with all problems and dilemmas that a typical student in school faces. It gives prime importance to psychology which is concerned with the changes and functioning of the mind of boys and girls. Thinking from a much more broadened view, it is a prerequisite for a teacher to handle transgender students too who really face traumas and depression in their life.

Teachers should be respectful and inclusive of all students' individual learning identities. Gender identity and associated topics have to be included in the curricula of training teachers so that all budding teachers will gain a deeper understanding of how to engage with these students in a manner that is respectful, inclusive and positive. To support a student who undergoes a mental strain in getting into terms with its gender identity is not an easy nut to crack until and unless we know about them. It needs patience and authentic knowledge only then the students can be properly guided. Teachers should be made to have an open mind to get into a transparent communication, only through which the real problems of the students can be tracked.

Yet another very curious and thought-provoking issue is that students must be confused within a classroom environment if their peers disclose that they identify themselves as transgenders. There will be students who are even not aware of what in fact transgender and gender transition are. When encountering such situations, teachers should have the presence of mind to reassure the students that they too deserve the same respect and courtesy that they would extend to any other person. Other students may have questions about the students who have identified themselves as transgenders, particularly when they undergo transition while at the same school. Teachers should be provided with a suggested response to the questions as it is not very easy to handle. Providing a safe and supportive learning environment is the sole responsibility of the teachers who are the guiding spirits.

A sample plan to deal with these situations effectively has to be incorporated into the curriculum of B.Ed. as it is high time that the traditional curricular structure has to be revised and updated. With the advancements in the world, a world that prioritizes individuals, anything that violates the basic dignity of individuals has to be tackled systematically. The physical, mental, social and emotional development of not only boys and girls but also trans students has to be included in the domain of psychology of the curricular structure of training teachers. Even though the strategies included in it could not be applied to all circumstances, the teacher will get an overall idea of how to cope with the diverse situations. The actual strategies will vary according to their individual circumstances and the school which they attend.

Teaching about gender identity and expression and the psychology of transgender students has to be considered as a part of a healthy curriculum. The curriculum should also be included with experiences of the students who have faced gender-based marginalization and violence. This could be an eye-opener to many of the trainee teachers to make an effective decision to deal with these darkened problems once they step into the profession of teaching. As teachers, they should try to develop a completely student-centred approach if any of the students is misgendered or misidentified within the classroom. An entirely different approach has to be taken if someone tries to violate the dignity of these students deliberately or frequently.

A teacher who very well knows gender identity can give insights into their experiences, individual competencies, goals and the like. Having self-awareness about various gender-related problems can help in cultivating a gender-inclusive classroom for the students. teachers should always be very much careful while using expressions, examples, activities etc within the classroom as it should never ignore and hinder the basic rights of the students. The teachers can also expose the students to real-life incidents pertaining to gender-related issues. It is not at all easy to handle all these situations and that is where the importance of updating the curriculum of teachers finds significance.

Inclusive education in the curriculum should also look up at gender, sex, identity crisis, non-conformity etc as it will help to gap the bridge between the traditional stigmas associated with these topics and the very real reality. There is in fact no generalized principles on how to deal with transgender students but awareness about these groups of children surely helps the teacher to be equipped with strategies to manage any situations that come before them.

CONCLUSION

Education is something that is a very powerful weapon to fight against all sorts of atrocities and irregularities. The scope of education is so vast that it can change the whole world into a better place. Schools are the media through which education is imparted to the young aspiring minds with the help of the light-bearers, the teachers. Schools with a set of teachers and the administrative setup should be committed to providing a safe and engaging learning environment that is free from all sorts of violence, harassment, marginalization and discrimination. All students are to be valued equally without discernment. Teachers play a very significant role in helping them and they need to be trained effectively especially when it comes to transgender students. Gender-inclusive education and the subsequent effective strategies to win the minds of those children to help and guide children who are in need of it has to be included in the curriculum. It has become now a very important need that the B.Ed. the curriculum has to be updated as it is essential to accept and understand these students. Since, transgenders have not fully acquired independence and autonomy, and are still under the threats of various atrocities and identity crises, the need to talk about these issues continue to be a matter of prime importance and that need to be addressed in the most effective way. Education plays a rejuvenating spirit in cleansing the minds of society. Thus, for tackling the perplexities of young aspiring minds in school, teachers have to be prepared well with all possible approaches.

REFERENCE

Campos, David. (2018). *Understanding Transgender Students. Helping Transgender Students Feel Accepted Starts with Understanding.* Retrieved from https://www.nsba.org/ASBJ/Past-Issues/June/Understanding-transgender-students /full-on 6/02/22

Padanna, Ashraf. (2016). *India Opens First School for Transgender Students in India.* Retrieved fromhttps://www.bbc.com/news/world-asia-india on 7/02/22

Rajdev, Bhumika. (2020). *For Transgender Persons, Discrimination Begins at School.* Retrieved from https://thewire.in/lgbtqia/cbse-results-transgender-students-education-stigma-discrimination on 7/02/22

Wadhawan, Adhitya.(2021). *Easing the Inclusion of Transgender Students in School.* Retrieved fromhttps://timesofindia.indiatimes.com/home/education/news/easing-the-inclusion-of-transgender-students-in-schools/articleshow/88028667.cms

BIO-NOTE

Archa Gopan is pursuing B.Ed. Degree in English from KTCT College of Teacher Education, Kaduvayil, Thiruvananthapuram, University of Kerala. My research interest lies in the field of Gender Studies. She completed her Bachelor's Degree in English Language and Literature from NSS College, Nilamel, University of Kerala. Then, she earned her post-graduate degree in English Language and Literature from Mar Ivanios College, Nalanchira, University of Kerala. She also did six months certificate course in Teaching English as a Second Language from IGNOU. She also has an interest in reading, content making, writing articles and the like.

CHAPTER X

GENDER SENSITIZATION TO FOSTER PARITY: ROLE OF EDUCATORS AS SYNERGISTS

Feba Mary Sabu

ABSTRACT

The process of changing the stereotypical concept or notion in order to modify behaviour by culturing awareness of gender equality is gender sensitization. Without being sensitive to a particular gender, an individual may withhold from understanding the opposite gender and in some cases even himself or herself. The need for this sensitivity has been felt and realised from times immemorial and in almost all kinds of human existence, across the globe. Education serves as an essential tool to bridge the gap between the genders and banish stereotypical notions. Educational institutions and educators can actively prove to be the decisive factors and act as synergists in promoting gender sensitization.

This paper considers that gender sensitization seeks to question and subsequently change the very thought-process of gender disparity, and it aims to initiate a sense of empathy and acceptance towards the other gender. It further tries to analyse the role of educators as synergists in enabling students to examine their own perceptions and attitudes which ultimately help in shaping a just and unprejudiced society.

Keywords: Gender Sensitization, Parity, Synergy and Stereotype.

• • •

RELEVANCE OF THE STUDY

Gender equality is not only a fundamental human right but a necessary pedestal for a peaceful, prosperous and sustainable future. However, a large part of the system and a large segment of our population is not really sensitive to this gender concern. Educators could be instrumental in shaping the gender-sensitive minds of the future. This could be made possible by reviewing the factors affecting discrimination and thus concretizing the strategies of educators to foster parity among individuals in a classroom.

METHODOLOGY

The research method of the study is a descriptive research and it attempts to comprehend the need for gender sensitization in order to foster parity. It reviews the role of educators as the synergist in this process. The research tool used is content analysis and the qualitative aspects of the research study are reiterated. This study is perfected by dint of secondary data. Secondary sources of data used are (a) journals, (b) scholarly articles, (c) research papers, (d) newspapers (e) books and other academic publications.

INTRODUCTION

According to WHO, sex refers to biological and physiological characteristics that define men and women. In simpler terms, it states the anatomy an individual is born with. Although, gender according to WHO refers to the socially constructed roles, behaviours, activities, and attributes that a given society considers appropriate for men and women. A major difference between sex and gender is that sex is biologically determined, whereas an individual chooses the gender they wish to identify as.

Gender is not a binary concept but a spectrum. Gender sensitization could be viewed as a process of equipping the society in order to instil empathy into the views that one hold about one's own sex and that of others. It acquaints men and women with each other's existence and helps to generate respect for the individual regardless of sex.

Education enables people to use and extend their capabilities, develop skills, improve their livelihoods and increase their earning potential. And it also empowers them to participate in decision-making and transform their lives and societies. As an educator, this could be made possible by nurturing students' own expressive energy and acting as a synergist in this process.

Unlike sex, gender is more amorphous in nature and is subject to change with reference to context and time. Hence, it keeps on changing from context to context and it serves as a major challenge. Gender is a political view of sex that is based on the binary division of male and female. This binary diffusion apparently looks natural but the problem begins when one is considered inferior to the other and this further give rise to many other problems in the society. Gendered assumptions and gender-based social discriminations exist throughout society, from organisational planning to everyday interactions at the workplace. Negative impacts of such assumptions can undermine the efficiency and success of even the best-intentioned plans. Gender sensitization training is the practical tool for analysing gender relations and provides adequate information regarding major factors that influence and are responsible for maintaining or changing the structure of gender relations.

In a country like India with vast diversity, so-called 'gender roles' are deep-rooted into the nerves and veins.

Customs, traditions, rituals, social values, family beliefs and individual perceptions are in need of a more systematic, well planned and more professional approach in order to inculcate the sensitivity towards gender and primarily highlight the contribution of both the genders in the creation and development of a well-balanced society.

I. FACTORS THAT PAVE WAY FOR GENDER DISCRIMINATION

Gender discrimination, starting from the prenatal stage, continues to rob children of their childhood and limit their chances until grave– disproportionately affecting the whole world. Disparities between the genders are prohibited by law, however, it still holds ground in every facet of society. Despite worldwide progress in eliminating them, gender inequality persists. The COVID-19 pandemic has threatened to put years of hard-won progress at risk.

Far too many girls, especially those from the poorest families, still face gender discrimination in education, child marriage and pregnancy, sexual violence and unrecognized domestic work. Boys are also forced to bear the burden of the family after a certain age, without any sort of emotional burst out.

Robert Blum, in his paper for 'Global Early Adolescent Study', shows the need for unbuttoning the 'gender straitjackets' as he found children in his study as extremely conservative and they truly believed that woman's personality is associated with vulnerability whereas man's associated with independence.

Following are the factors that lead towards gender discrimination;

SOCIETAL FACTORS

Male dominance and the dominant ideology of patriarchy: Most countries have a strong patriarchal custom, where men hold authority over the female family members and inherit property. This custom where inheritance passes from father to son is prevalent in India.

Education: Female literacy rate of the developed country are satisfying while the ranking position of the developing and underdeveloped countries are not good. Even before the pandemic, girls were more likely than boys to never set foot in a classroom. This is a grim reality in many parts of the world. Conflict, poverty and other forms of social disadvantages also magnify gender inequality in education.

Gender-based violence: Gender-based violence such as rape, sexual assault, an insult to modesty, kidnapping, abduction, cruelty by intimate partner or relatives, importation or trafficking of both boys and girls, persecution for dowry, indecency and all other crimes are ubiquitous.

Dowry: The dowry system in our society also contributes to gender discrimination by influencing the perception that girls are a burden on families.

Child marriage: Child marriage is a form of gender-based violence and a driver of gender inequality and gender discrimination. Experts predict that the COVID-19 pandemic is set to reverse 25 years of progress, which saw child marriage rates decline. In fact, Save the Children analysis revealed a further 2.5 million girls at risk of marriage by 2025 because of the pandemic—the greatest surge in child marriage rates in nearly three decades.

Child labour: There are currently 152 million children engaged in child labour around the world. Child labour makes it difficult for children to attend a school or limits their attendance, putting them at risk of falling behind their peers. Boys and girls are affected differently by child labour and parents' decisions are often influenced by wider social norms about the different roles that they should play in the home and in society. Girls are much more likely to shoulder the responsibility for household chores while boys are more likely to engage in harmful work such as construction. Girls are usually pulled out of school earlier than boys and causing wastage and stagnation in the field of education.

CULTURAL FACTORS

Religious practices: Religious rituals are reserved to be performed by males for their parents' afterlife. Priesthood and other leadership roles in a religious framework are exclusively reserved for men in many cases.

Gender-specific dress code: Every culture has a definite dress code designed for both boys and girls, starting from colour and type. This very idea is instilled into the minds of children and cause many other problems in society.

Predisposition to prefer son: In our male dominant, boys are given the exclusive rights to inherit the family name and properties and they are viewed as additional status for their family.

In Decision Making: Women have less authority than men to legal recognition and protection, as well as lower access to public knowledge and information, and less decision-making power both within and outside the home. This is also one of the reasons for gender discrimination.

ECONOMIC FACTORS

Labour participation: There is wage inequality between men and women in the workplace. A substantial number of women enter the labour market after their thirties, generally after completion of their reproductive roles of childbearing and rearing.

Access to credit: There are large disparities between men and women in terms of status and access to the workplace.

Property Rights: Although women have equal rights under the law to own property and receive equal inheritance rights, while, women are at a disadvantage in their practical life.

Employment inequality: Some common inequalities which also take place in the workplace are the gender-based imbalances of individuals in power and command over the management of the organization. Women are not able to move up into higher paid positions quickly as compared to men.

These factors are common and responsible for gender discrimination and many more factors influence to drive the discrimination. It also varies from society to society, according to their social atmosphere.

II. NEED FOR SENSITIZATION TO FOSTER PARITY

Gender sensitization is a movement through which the people with stereotypical concepts and traditional thought processes, are transformed and equipped to assure equal participation of women and men in decision-making; to facilitate equally; to equally access the resources; to acquire alike benefits of development; to get equal opportunities in employment; and also, can get equivalent regard in all other aspects of their life and livelihood so that both genders can enjoy life in its fullest.

Particularly in a country like India, with the vast diversity existing in terms of its customs, beliefs, traditions, rituals, skills, values, and individualistic perception, the need for a more systematic, planned and more professional approach is desired to inculcatethis sensitivity and primarily highlight the contribution of both the genders in creation and development of a well-balanced society.

When children are empowered to lead their lives, speak their minds and determine their futures, everyone benefits. History suggests that when we fight gender oppression, societies become more stable, safe and prosperous, with happier, better-educated citizens.

III. EDUCATORS PLAYING THE ROLE OF A SYNERGIST

Gender issues are prevailing in the society in every facet of life. In order to minimize these gender issues, we need to initiate changing the mindset of the younger generations of society as they are those who can bring about further change in society with their innovative ideas, thoughts and practices. So as to attain this, we are in need of educators, who have a vision for their mission to eliminate gender disparities. Teachers play a very important role in the early upbringing of the child and their ideas and beliefs can change the thought patterns and thus create an impact on young minds. A teacher must, therefore, constantly be aware of the fact that his or her actions, attitude, behaviour, perspective, approach, manner, outlook and mindset will definitely help to shape a child's personality. The teacher may use multiple strategies and interventions to ensure that students have equal opportunities to both create and obtain their goals.

According to the mission statement of the United Nations Decade of Education for Sustainable Development (ESD), "Teachers are strategically positioned to act as agents of change in order to achieve gender equality, especially through what they teach, how they teach and how they role model their own attitudes, beliefs and practices in the classroom and beyond. Indeed, teachers do not come into classrooms as gender-neutral persons. They are likely to have internalized a patriarchal gender ideology through their upbringing and years of socialization in both formal and informal settings. This paper uses experiential, interactive, participatory and reflective methodologies to sensitize students to the classroom practice implications of gender consciousness so that teachers can adopt a gender perspective in their everyday lives and in their teaching functions."

Teachers are required to be serious about the gender issue. In order to equip the teachers to bring about a change in society, they should primarily have a pre-set knowledge of the issue. Teachers need not only gender-sensitive curriculum and textbooks but also gender equality education. Teachers can serve as role models for the students. When children are supported to be active in civic and political spaces irrespective of their gender, in particular, they are empowered with the tools and skills to be the drivers of positive change in their families and communities.

IV. STRATEGIES TO BE EMPLOYED IN A CLASSROOM

Through Gender Sensitization a cordial and amiable environment could be developed in the classrooms where there is mutual respect and trust between the sexes, without sexual innuendoes and obstructive chauvinism to blemish the atmosphere. Teachers play a very important role in the early upbringing of a child. Children in the formative years easily nurture values and virtues taught to them. Gender-sensitive training should be made mandatory for teachers. The training will enable them to disseminate the desirable attitude based on mutual respect and trust between girls and boys.

The classroom has to be embodied in such a way as to effectuate gender sensitization. Certain strategies that could be followed in the classroom to foster parity are listed below;

- **Maintaining a Clear Set of Rules:** It is important to establish a well-defined set of rules in the classroom to promote equity among pupils. Respecting sex differences and embracing gender equality should be fostered.
- **Including Group Activities:** Heterogeneous groups should be formed for the group activity. Ideas from all the pupils are encouraged and accepted in this setup. All are prompted to think freely without any inhibition and discuss their ideas with their peers.
- **Promoting Gender Neutral Dress Code:** Gender-neutral dressing just aims to eliminate gender-based oppression, inequalities and also violence at times.
- **Planning Mixed Seating Arrangement:** Pupils could be made to seat without any sort of gender differences. Mixed seating plans should be established so as to nurture mutual respect and care.
- **Using Gender-Neutral Language:** Teachers can also change the language within the lessons in order to help students to expand perspectives beyond gender stereotypes.

CONCLUSION

Eradicating gender issues would create a world where every gender enjoys equal rights, resources, opportunities and protections. It is imperative to discard the pre-established roles and positions of different genders and spend the days not thinking about how to fit in a certain 'role'. The education sector could certainly play a pivotal role in eliminating gender inequality. It is important to know that the inclusion of the concept of gender equality in the curriculum and the making of laws to remove gender inequality have a significant impact on the need to achieve the constitutional goal of establishing an egalitarian society.

The limitations of the study cannot be overlooked as the central domain of sex or gender-sensitive research is the dissimilitude between sex and gender. Although the terms 'sex' and 'gender' denote different aspects of being male and female, they are often used interchangeably in the literature and it creates clutter. Moreover, the National Curriculum Framework (2005) document recognized that:

"We must use textbooks as one of the primary instruments for equality since for a great majority of school-going children, as also for teachers, it is the only accessible and affordable resource for education" (Panday 2004).

However, the textbooks remain to spread gender-biased ideas into society. The concept and spreading of sexism take its root from the negative representations in textbooks. It is quite clear that despite an explicit policy of gender sensitization of school curriculum, the situation on the ground did not improve a great deal. Gender disparity is only one facet of a much larger issue of equity within education. However, by making efforts to break down traditional gender roles in the classroom, we can better prepare students to seek knowledge and participate more fully in discussions and other learning opportunities in many fields, regardless of their gender. Ultimately, it is the change in social mindset and involvement of all sections of society that is required to achieve the ends. If we wish to create skilled, globalised, effective human capital based on a revived education system, we cannot afford to discriminate between the genders and leave any of them behind at the facets of life.

WORKS CITED

Blum, R. W. (2017, October). It Begins at 10: How Gender Expectations Shape Early Adolescence Around the World. *The Journal of Adolescent Health.*

Trivedi, T. (2012, January 1). *Gender Sensitization.* Jnanada Prakashan.

Vasundhara, S. (2020). Importance of Gender Sensitization. *International Journal of Multidisciplinary and Current Educational Research, 2*(5), pp. 120-125.

BIONOTE

A self-motivated person with an enthusiastic and determined mind in the academic and cultural realm. She completed her Bachelor's Degree in Economics from Madras Christian College and currently, a teacher educand at Titus II Teachers College, Tiruvalla.

CHAPTER XI

HEGEMONIC MASCULINITY, MARGINALIZATION AND DOMESTIC VIOLENCE: A LOOKING INTO AFRICAN WOMEN'S LIFE THROUGH BUCHI EMECHETA AND CHIMAMANDA NGOZI ADICHIE

Ambili P.

Abstract

Why was Africa called the black continent? Europeans were behind this agenda; they were not ready to recognize them. The geographical features and their skin tone fixed the name. So, they were marginalized from the mainstream and compelled to be slaves of the white. When an African man suppress these ways, what will be the condition of an African woman? They marginalized different ways from different sections. Writers from Africa started their writing to express reality to the outside world. Feminist ideology helped women writers to raise their voice because feminism is an interdisciplinary approach to the issues of equality based on gender, gender expression, identity and sex. Why feminism is as relevant as before? The one and the only reason is hegemonic masculinity and the monopoly of men. Raewyn Connell's concept of "Hegemonic Masculinity" serves as an analytical instrument to identify those attitudes and practices among men that perpetuate gender inequality, involving both men's domination over women. There are multiple forms of masculinity to be found in every society such as hegemonic masculinity, complicit masculinity, marginalized masculinity. In complicit masculinity, a man may not fit into all the characteristics of hegemonic masculinity, but do not challenge it either. Since they are not challenging the systems of gender that are present in our societies, they do receive some benefits from being male. When we come to Africa, feminism is somewhat different from other regions. Their women are facing triple marginalization. The first one is marginalized from the nation, the second one is gender-based and the third one is class-based which is by women on women. A woman with good social respect and orders gains their power over the ordinary ones.

Keywords: Hegemonic Masculinity, Marginalization, Feminism, Africa.

• • •

Ali A Mazrui and others mention seven conflicts as themes of African writings such as the clash between past and present, the tradition and modernity, indigenous and foreign, between individualism and community, socialism and capitalism, development and self-reliance and between Africanity and humanity. The triple marginalization theory was developed by black socialists in the united states such as Claudia Jones. In the context of the global black struggle, there have been many women who fought against the white supremacist system and who have been erased from the historical narratives. And also, there has been a culture of gendered silence that has accompanied being a woman in the revolution. That black solidarity requires the silence of black women. They require black women to be silent in their life. Most African writers consider writings are a medium to express their life and realities through creativity. When we come to African women writers, they are also focusing on struggles and atrocities they faced especially gender issues. Ama Ata Aidoo, Buch Emecheta, Chimamanda Adichie etc. are some of the popular feminist writers in African literature.

Buchi Emecheta is one of Nigeria's early prominent female writers. Her succussed life has created a path of inspiration for contemporary Nigerian women writers. Her works reveal Nigerian female characters who challenge the prescribed notions of their roles as 'women', 'wife', and 'mother'. Emecheta uses her own personal experiences as the stepping stone in expressing and confronting female subjugation. The main source of inspiration for her writing was the village of Ibusa in Eastern Nigeria where her family came from. Even though she had spent a relatively brief period of her childhood there, the villages and the stories she heard on her visits with her mother left an indelible mark on the young girl and become the lodestone for all she wrote. In "The slave girl ", "The Bride Price "and "The Joys of Motherhood", she poignantly captured, in a manner reminiscent of her male contemporary Chinua Achebe, a vanishing Igbo culture in the process of transition to modernity.

Emecheta's feminism was deeply inscribed in her identity as an African woman with African values. Her books "In the Ditch", "Second class Citizen", "The Bride prize", "The Slave Girl", "The Joys of Motherhood" and many others covered themes such as the marginalization of women and girls, patriarchal oppression, racism, poverty, social exclusion and all the real-life experiences she shared through characters in her books. "Head Above Water" is her autobiography. Emecheta's feminism is very clear through her writing, most of her works focused on the unfair treatment of women in traditional, rural, urban and modern settings. In the life of African women education takes second place, marriage is a prior thing. In this enclosed space, every woman is to fight for her survival as an individual and also overcome the cruel practice of marginality. Through marriage they think, a woman attains a status acclaimed by society and fulfils her biological needs of procreation and companionship. "The Joys of Motherhood" is Emecheta's one of the most acclaimed novels. The novel goes through a traditional Igbo woman Nnu Ego and her battle with accepting the new culture of Lagos without abandoning her native culture. When Igbo culture focuses on patriarchy, marriage, children etc. Lagos gives priority to individual success and money. Actually, all the women are compelled to face a dilemma that whether family or self-require more priority here, Nnu Ego is also trapped between these two separate belief systems. Emecheta says that patriarchy, capitalism and native traditions affects one's life and also some other operating oppressive factors what she mentioned in her "The Joys of Motherhood". The first operating factor is Nnu Ego's second husband Nnaife and how lack of an Igbo identity affects their marriage, other factors are the second world war and Christianity. Emecheta's second novel "Second class Citizen" portrays a character almost different from Nnu Ego, because the main character, Adah is said to be based on Emecheta herself. Her perspectives of an African Woman's life in a patriarchal and marginalized society are very clear here.

At one stage, Nnu Ego thinks that if she were in Ibuza she would have her own hut and be given respect: in colonized Lagos she had to face polygamy and exploitation. There are many similarities between Emecheta and Adah. Here Emecheta shows how a woman tries to overcome patriarchy because it gives hope. Through feminist view, patriarchy is frequently considered to be the main factor to oppress a woman all over the world. In her "The bride price" she explores the role of myth through the life of Akunna a young bride who is haunted by the fear of death during childbirth as her bride price was not paid. Emecheta's novels provide an insight into the weakness and misconception in women themselves which tend to perpetuate their humiliation and subjugation.

When we go through these two authors, it is very clear that the motive is common that is both Emecheta and Adiche have tried to express reality what happens in Africa. They focus on women and their condition in society and also portray their own life through different characters. Chimamanda Ngozi Adichie is a Nigerian author whose works drew extensively on the Biafran war in Nigeria during the late 1960s. As a student at Eastern Connecticut State University, she began writing her first novel" Purple Hibiscus", set in Nigeria and it is the coming-of-age story of Kambili, fifteen years old whose family is wealthy and well respected but she is terrorized by her fanatically religious father. 'Purple Hibiscus' garnered the commonwealth writer's prize in 2005 for the best book. In this novel, Kambili's world is circumscribed by the high walls and frangipani trees of her family compound. Her wealthy Catholic father, under whose shadow Kambili lives, while generous and politically active in the community, is repressive and fanatically religious at home. When Nigeria begins to fall apart under a military coup, Kambili's father sends her and her brother away to stay with their aunt Ifeoma, a university professor, whose house is noisy and full of laughter. There Kambili and her brother discover a new life and love beyond the confines of their father's authority.

Here, why Kambili and their brother feel happy with their aunt? They suffered especially women members in most of the family's maltreatment in many ways whether it is domestic or public violence. In 'Purple Hibiscus 'the powerful narrator, Kambili Achike who together with her mother and brother all the victims of domestic violence of the patriarch in the family. Even her mother Beatrice lives in fear of Eugene's wrath as he controls almost every aspect of their lives. The members of the family cannot voice out their feelings freely. Here, Adichie tries to show the tyrannical, wicked and hypothetical Eugene Achike and how he rules. Eugene is one of the best examples of the patriarchal way of life found in most of the families in Africa. Actually, it is not only in the case of African life but all over the world. In a family, the life of a wife and children focus on the male authority. But when we come into the black community, the women are marginalized triply.

Through Beatrice, Adichie showed how wives are oppressed by their husbands. Beatrice is a "good wife" Africa calls, because, she obeys her husband all the time. She doesn't have her own time and happiness. There are a lot of examples to show Eugene's brutal behaviours towards his wife. Once Beatrice happens to feel nausea and dizziness which makes her ask their husband's permission to Waite and rest in the car instead of joining their family to see father Benedict, but he didn't like that, so she decided to follow him bearing the pain silently. Even though she follows her husband's orders she is brutally beaten at home, that's why she suffers a miscarriage. Not only Beatrice but Kambili and Jaja, her brother also physically oppressed by their father. Kambili remains unconscious for several days and is hospitalized as a result of this cruel attack.

Here, Adichie has tried to show the other woman who has the courage to raise her voice against oppression through Ifeoma, Eugene's sister. She is strong, bold and self-depended. Here, Ifeoma advised Beatrice to pull her out of disastrous marriage, then only she thinks independently and quit domestic abuse. The end of the novel shows the reality and the true picture of a wife's tolerance. Because Papa died suddenly, the autopsy reveals he has been poisoned. And Mama tells Kambili and Jaja that she had been feeding poison to Papa, this is the result of all her sufferings and intolerance. But when the police arrive, Jaja confesses to the crime, but Mama influenced lawyers and bribed to ease Jaja's time in jail. There is another character that is Sisi, Maidservant of Beatrice who helps Beatrice to leave the struggling life. Beatrice is very close to Sisi and who gave poison to kill Eugene. This is the case of a woman helping other women to end oppression. The character of Beatrice and Ifeoma is the best example of two types of women in our society.

Adichie's other work "Americanah" also highlight these things such as marginalization and other problems faced by women. Americanah is an award-winning novel about a young Nigerian woman, Ifemelu, who immigrates to the United States where she struggles with racism, relationships and identity. When we go through the life of Ifemelu we can understand that there is a hidden agenda behind the lives in America, that is Americanization. It mainly focuses on African immigrants and racial problems. Although her "Half of a yellow sun "doesn't show the conflict between man and woman relationship, it shows the agency of feminist works. It encounters the aforementioned author's assumption that war is predominantly male experience through the female characters' active participation in the Biafran war. When we go through these two authors, it is very clear that the motive is common that is both Emecheta and Adiche have tried to express reality what happens in Africa. They focus on women and their condition in society and also portray their own life through different characters.

Works Cited

*Connell, R.W Gender and Power: Society, the person and sexual politics. Palo Alto, CA: Stanford University Press

* Emecheta B The joys of Motherhood Heinemann Educational Publishers1979

* Emecheta, Buchi, Second class Citizen, Heinemann Educational Publishers 1974

*Cox, C. Brian, ed. African writers.: Charles Scribner's Sons,1997

*Adichie, Chimamanda Ngozi. Purple Hibiscus: A Novel. London: Forth Estate,2003.

AN ANALOGY OF THE PERVASIVE FEELING IN THE POEMS OF HEALING, AN ANTHOLOGY OF LOCKDOWN POEMS PUBLISHED BY UN AND KYRIE

Meera K. S.

Abstract

This study aims at the inscape of some lockdown poems from the anthology, *The Poems of Healing* written by poets from various parts of the world and a mosaic of sonnets titled *Kyrie,* which was written by Ellen Bryant Voigt. . This research mainly focuses on the selected poets' Invictus self-esteem to rebuild a positive and hopeful ambience in their poems, although they are named as 'lockdown poems'. The sonnets in *Kyrie* launch the readers straightaway into the centre of the pandemic: "everybody's dying and there's nothing you can do".

Keywords: lockdown poetry, pervasive feeling, hope, optimism.

• • •

An Analogy of the Pervasive Feeling in *The Poems of Healing*, an Anthology of Lockdown Poems Published by UN and *Kyrie*, a Sonnet Sequence by Ellen Bryant Voigt based on the 1918 Pandemic

Lockdown poetry is a new genre of poetry, that emerged after the arrival of COVID 19. As the people are fed up with the terms quarantine, mask, sanitiser, there evolved a deviation into new creative lifestyles. In order to promote such talents, the United Nations collected a list of poems from the nook and corner of the world, brought out as *The Poems of Healing*. Although these poems are the outcome of disturbed minds, made by the tragic consequences of Coronavirus, they are not pessimistic at all. Ellen Bryant Voigt's book-length sonnet sequence, *Kyrie*, remains one of the major works about the 1918 influenza pandemic. Voigt's poetry has reflected her endless quest to unite her two artistic impulses: music and storytelling, and her work as a whole recite her need and "will to change". Both the settings and characters in the poems imply the local but her major concern is universal: "choice and fate, and the tension between them that constitutes human life.

An overtone of optimism can be negotiated from the deeper layer of the semantic realm of the poems in the anthology *The Poems of Healing*. The world-renowned writer Victor Hugho says: "Even the darkest night will end and the sun will rise", in his magnum opus *Les Miserables*. Likewise, these poets declare a new rising of the ached people from an anguished situation to glorious ordinary life. It is too soon to tell whether this one will usher in that kind of sustained growth, but there are reasons for optimism.

The last great pandemic, the 1918 influenza outbreak, was followed by the Roaring Twenties. *Kyrie* is a book-long sequence of rough, unrhymed sonnets that vary considerably in syntax and in rhetorical emphasis. Some speak in the first person, some are letters home, while others speak through the third person. To personalise the influenza pandemic of 1918, Voigt engages in various literary devices. The title, "Kyrie", is derived from the Greek word "O Lord", and the rather common name is associated with Christian prayer. The title echoes a personal prayer and serves to symbolise the circumstances of the characters in the poems.

Crises always lead people to find new ways to do things, adopt new technologies and cast away old practices. In the United States, the ability of large parts of the economy to function and excel in the digital realm when the physical economy was broadly shut down, has surprised even techno-optimists. Everyone has a choice in how he or she thinks about any situation that is to be faced. Radical optimism is the notion that there's an upside to everything. Even a global pandemic and worldwide health crisis. Moreover, optimism is essential for mental well-being in a crisis that needs action.

Optimism is a part of psychology that is categorized into hyponyms and also the definition of optimism an understanding of everything that is good and pleasant and an attitude always has good expectations. Optimism is the quality of being full of hope and emphasizing the good parts of a situation or belief that something good will happen according to the Cambridge dictionary (2019). Goleman (2002) stated optimism is a strong hope in everything that is contained in life that will be able to overcome well, even though there are problems. Furthermore, optimism is a good hope that someone has for everything that happens in life even though they are in trouble.

This study concentrates mainly on the selected fifty lockdown poems in the anthology, *The Poems of Healing,* published by the United Nations in the year 2021. The selected poems are 'As the Snow' by Silvia Mssardi, 'Frosty Beginnings' by Davida Eyam- Ozung, 'I am the Forest' by Md. Firoj Alam, 'Journey of Life' by Ilhem Brini,' Let the

Birds Fly' by Kumari. S. Wickramasinghe, 'Deep Sad Feeling' by Ruth M Kemigisha and so on. These poets invariably exhibit a tendency to rebuild a brave new world from the frozen one, which was resulted from the pandemic. They exhibit perceptible commonality in displaying the optimistic tone in their lines. This study proposes to compare these poems with *Kyrie* by Voigt and examine what is their pervasive feeling and how hope and optimism play an important role in creating a Panglossian world.

The whole world is in a critical situation in which many people can not foresee their immediate future. *The poems of Healing* consists of poems from various walks of the world that may be examined in the light of the above ideas so as to interpret them as a result of potent mindsets. There are chances to fall into large trenches of emotional breakdown in this post covid era. This research mainly focuses on the selected poets' Invictus self-esteem to rebuild a positive and hopeful ambience in their poems, although they are named as 'lockdown poems'. The sonnets in *Kyrie* launch the readers straightaway into the centre of the pandemic: "everybody's dying and there's nothing you can do". This sense of helplessness reflects the breakdown of social order and introduces the notion of social death. Since time immemorial, social death succeeded physical death with its social aspect of death being marked by rites like funerals and wakes. Yet, if metaphorically speaking one is considered dead, or "as good as dead," social death precedes biological death.

Both hope and optimism emerge from a combination of genetic, cultural, environmental, and historical factors. Hope is a stable individual state of mind that is event-specific, depends on external situations, and includes a successful sense of agency and pathways. Optimism is a character trait or strength that is event-independent, does not depend on external situations, and in which individuals expect desired outcomes to happen in the future and undesired outcomes not to happen. Martin Seligman, regarded as the Father of Positive Psychology, found an optimistic explanatory style is a trainable skill rather than an inborn trait. The research evolves from two questions.

a. What is the pervasive feeling of the poems contained in the anthology, The Poems of Feeling and the sonnet sequence Kyrie?

b. How the idea of hope and optimism are conveyed through these poems?

The proposed research work attempts to investigate the pervasive feeling in the lockdown poems published by the UN and the sonnet sequence *Kyrie*. The selected works will be compared with each other with reference to their tone of hope and optimism. The radical optimism is to be analysed by determining the socio-political and cultural context of these poets. Moreover, the study will explore the ways in which the discourse of optimism helps the reader to be empathetic with that. In the contemporary context of depression, confusion and anxiety, how these poems prove to be sites of reframing the destroyed, will be looked into.

Optimism and hope are terms in positive psychology that a talent for joy, like any other, can be calculated. Martin Seligman is a pioneer of positive psychology (the term itself was coined by Abraham Maslow), not simply because he has a systematic theory about why happy people are happy, but because he uses the scientific method to explore it. Through the use of exhaustive questionnaires, Seligman found that the most satisfied, upbeat people were those who had discovered and exploited their unique combination of "signature strengths," such as humanity, temperance and persistence. This vision of happiness combines the virtue ethics of Confucius, Mencius and Aristotle with modern psychological theories of motivation. Seligman's conclusion is that happiness has three dimensions that can be cultivated: the Pleasant Life, the Good Life, and the Meaningful Life.

The Pleasant Life is realised if we learn to savour and appreciate such basic pleasures as companionship, the natural environment and our bodily needs. We can remain pleasantly stuck at this stage or we can go on to experience the Good Life, which is achieved through discovering our unique virtues and strengths and employing them creatively to enhance our lives. According to modern theories of self-esteem, life is only genuinely satisfying if we discover value within ourselves. Yet one of the best ways of discovering this value is by nourishing our unique strengths in contributing to the happiness of our fellow humans. Consequently, the final stage is the Meaningful Life, in which we find a deep sense of fulfilment by employing our unique strengths for a purpose greater than ourselves. The genius of Seligman's theory is that it reconciles two conflicting views of human happiness, the individualistic approach, which emphasises that we should take care of ourselves and nurture our own strengths, and the altruistic approach, which tends to downplay individuality and emphasizes sacrifice for the greater purpose.

The UN lockdown poetry collection, *The Poems of Healing*, begins with the following foreword:

Nurturing our mental health and well-being is more important than ever. United Nations personnel are committed to endlessly making a positive impact in our world. While this can be rewarding, it can take a toll on our mental health and well-being.

These words give a clear picture of the prevalent feeling of the selected poems.

Inspired by her father's childhood as an orphan during the 1918 pandemic, Voigt wanted to portray in *Kyrie* the irony of life. She had no particular interest in the pandemic, however, it occurred to her that her father's circumstances would resonate with many others who had survived it, its main victims have been young adults.

While acknowledging social breakdown, Voigt strives to provide a semblance of normality to a tumultuous and terrible time by employing a formal poetic form: the sonnet. The sonnet serves as a necessary tool to convey to its readers the enormity of this human tragedy and present it with an understandable context. *Kyrie* frames itself with readings of landscape in terms of former human presence. Like writing itself, the landscape retains only the faintest trace of what has gone before, but *Kyrie* commemorates the act of commemoration and reminds us how human emotion has already reified the p

The proposed research will proceed as an analytical enquiry where a comparative analysis of the selected writers will be made. The study will concentrate on how these poets from geographically distant places as well as culturally disparate occasions outline the post covid situation in their poems. The research will be based on the theory of hope and optimism, proposed by Martin Seligman, more specific is optimism values. The writer use a qualitative approach for this research. According to

Clissett (2008) qualitative research covers a wide range of approaches for the exploration of human experience, perception, motivations and behaviours and is concerned with the collection and analysis of words whether in the form of speech or writing. From the statement above, qualitative research is the form of research that includes human attitudes or experiences and motivations which are then analysed through words and writing.

In today's situation of covid 19, the people are depressed due to the after-effects of the pandemic in the socio-economic-cultural scenario. This study can prove the positive mindset of people from all walks of the world. The main effect of this study is to juxtapose the two different chronological periods and the corresponding literary works based on two pandemics. A positive outcome of the covid 19 was that the people could do many things which are considered as impossible or obscure. The poets from different regions, who write in different languages are to be analysed due to the commonality of the tone of their poems. With that, a sonnet sequence from a different time period based on another similar historical event can be analysed too.

Works Cited

Milić ,Danijela and Davis, Jack . *Sauti, The Poems of Healing*: US; 2020

Voigt, E. B. *Kyrie*. London: Norton;1995

Seligman, Martin E.P . *Learned Optimism: How to Change Your Mind and Your Life*. New York, NY: Pocket Books: 1991

Seligman, Martin E.P . *Authentic Happiness: Using the New Positive Psychology to Realize Your Potential for Lasting* Fulfilment. New York, NY: Free Press: 2002

BIO- NOTE

Meera K. S. is an academician who had completed her Post Graduation from Devamatha College, Kuravilangad. She took her B.Ed from St. Mary's College, Karikode. She is a former Guest Lecturer in the BPC College, Piravom and St. Mary's Training College, Karikode. She had cleared UGC NET. She is a guest lecturer at IHRD College, Njeezhoor. She has published articles in international journals such as IJCRT, IJRAR, PIJR. She also published a chapter in an ISBN book *Optima Scripta, Literarum Carmina, Indian English Poetry: A Critical Evaluation.* She has presented a paper at the national conference conducted by Kristu Jayanti College, Bengaluru and at the international conference conducted by NIT, Agartala.

CHAPTER XIII

PHILOSOPHY AND PSYCHOLOGY

S. PAVITHRA

M.Sc Psychology

ABSTRACT

Over the life span of human evolution, the journey to understand and outlook the human nature is a continuous process. The quest for a comprehensive understanding of the world was traced back to the sixth century. Philosophy is more of a way of thinking about questions. They relied on arguments and reasons and developed different branches of philosophy. But the great works of philosopher Rene Descartes is what makes philosophy exist till now. Philosophers slowly began to discuss the human mind. Even when psychology is separated from philosophy, both are contributing to each other, both spin around integrity, rationality and self. All existences in human life are there to widen our perspectives.

Over the life span of human evolution, the journey to understand and outlook the human nature is a continuous process. We are all in the oscillating swings on where to set our beliefs but the centre point emerges from thoughts of ideas. Our capacity to create and understand the meaning of ideas is considered to be an essential feature of human beings. These ideas formed into concepts and principles. These key circles operate the world of knowledge and let the people surf into the sea of exploration.

The quest for a comprehensive understanding of the world was traced back to the sixth century. But Philosophy traces its roots in ancient Greece. It came from the Greek word meaning love of wisdom. . Earlier, people explain the nature of the world through stories. When philosophical thoughts were emerging, scholars were tangled to find the distinction between science and storytelling. Then philosophers aimed to make sense of the human world and human experiences. They ponder over questions to understand what human life encounters. It began to revolve around where we find the value.

Philosophy is more of a way of thinking about questions. Philosophers relied on reason and arguments to explore the ideas as they do not have any specific methods for proving their theories. To test the statements they put forward, or they propose made-up situations and examine from different angles.

Philosophy has different branches of study which helps to understand different perspectives in the world. They are *metaphysics* – explains how one is related to other, *epistemology*- explain the theory of knowledge, *ethics*- asks what are moral beliefs and what makes a particular action right or wrong and *logic*- study the basic rules in persuasion while one argues. Logic is said to be a philosophers' toolbox. It answers the question in a clear, systematic way.

Even though the philosophical distinctions can be traced to Greeks, the great works of the philosopher are what makes them exist till now. Rene Descartes was the first to talk about the interactions of mind and body. Descartes stated that not only body can influence the mind, but that mind could also affect the body. Philosophers began to discuss the human mind. They ask whether the mind and soul are the same. Being aware of ourselves is called consciousness which is the central feature of the human mind. Some Philosophers ask where this awareness comes from. But Descartes's works caught the attention of others; his contributions have had a significant influence on psychology. And there began the work of William James and Wilhelm Wundt.

Wilhelm Wundt who is regarded as the father of psychology was first separated psychology from philosophy by his workings of the mind in a more structured way. His aim is to record the thoughts and sensations and analyse them to get the underlying structure. Basically, focus on understanding the process of organising the mind. He argued that the structure of the human mind can be studied scientifically using introspection. Even though it does not remain as a fundamental tool for a psychological explanation but this contribution showed that psychology could be valid as an experimental science field.

Even though psychology is separated from philosophy, both are contributing to each other and differ in approaches to each other. Some basic conceptual backgrounds are

Both philosophy and psychology explores the nature of humankind and their interactions. But Philosophy is the existential study that relies on the fundamental nature of knowledge, reality and existence. It actually makes the individual look at the world outside them. Philosophy provides us with valuable resources to our fundamental questions about life. On the other hand, Psychology is the field of study that relies on understanding human behaviour and neurological processes that guide mental wellbeing. It makes an individual have a look deep down inside themselves on how they interpret information through senses and how they react to life events.

Both philosophy and psychology helped to explain the importance of morality. Philosophy seeks everything which includes explaining the right ways of behaving. Even though psychology has proposed a variety of scales based on ethics and morality, it relied on what are the different morals that exist rather than right or wrong.

Philosophy has contributed some topics to psychology such as sensation, perception, intelligence, memory. Although both studying the same the answers they provide differs. The scientific researches have underlying general principles which fit philosophy into psychology. The end goal of philosophy has more intellectual purposes while psychology focuses on therapy and intervention.

It is said that philosophy is as wide as life; it travels around pondering questions and generating ideas. On the other hand, psychology is not merely a pure science. It has a highly practical side. But both philosophy and psychology spin around integrity, rationality and self. How we view ourselves, how we view the world, how we rationalise life happenings are intertwined by representing the reality of human life. In every aspect of our life, we think of the world as a place where we live in. what we value, why we value it, what we should about it and answers for these make sense to our existence. The philosophical things sprout best from the personal. We can never find world existing independent because every subjective reality is connected with world objectivities. All existences in human life are there to widen our perspectives.

Works cited

Illustrated family encyclopedia (2005), Dorling Kindersley Limited, London

https://www.classics.pitt.edu>research

www.ncertbooks.guru (Difference between philosophy and psychology)

exploringyourmind.com (relationship between philosophy and psychology)

<u>https://youtu.be/1A_CAkYt3GY</u> (what is philosophy)

Bio-Note

Ms Pavithra (M.Sc.) presently a freelance counsellor holds a post-graduate degree in psychology. She is a trained professional in counselling and psychotherapy and specialisation in art therapy. She published two articles, three poems and one short story. Currently getting trained in Forgiveness life coach certification programme.

CHAPTER XIV

THE OTHER SIDE OF MULTICULTURALISM: VIOLENCE IN GLORIA NAYLOR'S THE WOMEN OF BREWSTER PLACE

Aashlesha V. Lele

ABSTRACT

Multiculturalism can be defined based on its dual reception on the social front. The ideal utopian expectation remains a far-fetched dream in reality. The African American writer Gloria Naylor highlights this negative discourse of multiculturalism and sets her novel 'The Women of Brewster Place' in the typical multicultural background, presenting a diverse socio-cultural society. Along with highlighting the plight of the Women implicitly, the paper also thrives on bringing out the lopsided view of multiculturalism, issues of the multicultural society, the existential struggle and troubled experiences of 'the coloured folks', particularly black women. The paper essentially delves into the territory that presents the other side of multiculturalism, especially in the African American context, with predominant issues related to identity, sexuality, racism and psychological degeneration.

Keywords: Multiculturalism, Social Violence, Racism and Discourses of Multiculturalism.

INTRODUCTION

Multiculturalism as a concept is predominantly concerned with the diversity of perspectives. Like every moment and idea, multiculturalism too has various aspects and facets. Some advocating the positive stance view multiculturalism as a compatible seamless intermingling of different cultures while others consider it a utopian delusion - a potential threat to a coherent national identity and secularism, thereby fostering discrimination based on race, culture, ethnicity and colour. The present paper rejects the former ideas to solely focus on the negative aspects of multiculturalism in a particular socio-cultural community and in the desired coherent multicultural nation in general. Countries like Canada witnessed the success of multiculturalism, whereas the visible adverse effects of the same were experienced in Germany and United Kingdom. The impact of multiculturalism, both direct and indirect, can be seen in writers from various parts of the world, especially those living in multicultural societies. Focussing more on the undesirable aspects, this paper plans to study multiculturalism in an unfavourable setting, presenting it as a significant barrier to the coherent national identity, thereby leading to its fragmentation. This discussion will focus on how multiculturalism leads to violence, trauma and destruction.

The United States of America, a multicultural nation, is often referred to and interpreted as a "Salad Bowl", which has had a very traumatic past. Its traumatic history of slavery, racism and implementation of racial discrimination has hindered the nation's 'true assimilation'. In The Women of Brewster Place (1982), the African American novelist Gloria Naylor, focusing on the dominant feminist themes of the life and experiences of black women also deals with the issues of violence that seem to pose its roots on adversities of multiculturalism. Various episodes in the novel highlight the issue of violence which is seen manifesting itself through the complexities of multiculturalism, viewing its adverse effects that led to psychological distortions, identity crisis and physical abuse among the people of a particular ethnic group.

Through this fictional setting of Brewster place, the author is capable of successfully dealing with the real-life issues, retelling how the stings of racism and wounds of segregation have divided the human race, leading to destruction and degeneration. "Prejudice" according to Maya Angelou 'is a burden that confuses the past, threatens the future and renders the present inaccessible.' It won't be wrong to say that every writer from a multicultural background of 'the coloured' race expresses this burden of the past accompanied by confusion, chaos and unrest in his / her works. Speaking to Angels Carabi in one of the interviews, Gloria Naylor talked of her personal experience of racism and segregation which was felt in a direct manner in the South while in the North it was disguised in the air of subtlety, as she says "Racism here was more subtle" (24). In another interview with Ashford, speaking on the racial segregation of her nation the author says "I think we're still struggling under the scars of slavery, and I think that the Civil Rights Movement did not work. The country is almost as divided as before" (74-75).

The Trauma of Psychological Abuse

The novel witnesses one of intense psychological damage caused in the character of Kiswana Browne, a mixed-race offspring born of a white father and a black mother, a condition that pulled her still closer to experience a continuous clash of culture, both within and around her. Though she is an outcome of the union of black and white parents, she is always drawn towards the black. She celebrates and asserts her negritude and her being black. She knew that Black is something to do with negativity, yet she overlooks the fact and takes pride in everything that would contribute to her identity as a black. Regarding such obsessions with one's own identity, Amartya Sen in his book Identity and Violence: The Illusion of Destiny proclaims, "A sense of identity can be a source not merely of pride and joy, but also of strength and confidence" (Sen, 1).

The way in which Naylor presents the character of Kiswana is very interesting. Kiswana is of a light complexion with straight hair. Dissatisfied with her physical attributes, she is often seen complaining to her mother for her physical dissimilarity with her race that does not project her as a black. She actively participates in all sorts of revolutions for the emergence of black republicans in college. In order to resemble a 'negro' and achieve a sort of assimilation with her roots, she tries to curl her hair and even changes her original name Melanie to adopt a name that sounds more African– 'Kiswana'. Kiswana's conversations with her black mother, bring out her psychological rage and the emotional turmoil when she says, "Oh, God, I can't take this anymore. Trying to be something I'm not–trying to be something I'm not mama! Trying to be proud of my heritage and the fact that I was of African descent. If that's being what I'm not, then I say fine. But I'd rather be dead than be like you–a white man's nigger who's ashamed of being black!" (TWBP, 85)

Amartya Sen, also while discussing the negative aspects of such identical obsessions writes, "And yet identity can also kill and kill with abandon. A strong–and exclusive–sense belonging to one group can in many cases carry with it the perception of distance and divergence from other groups" (Sen, 1-2). This proves to be true in the case of Kiswana. Her obsessions about her identity and her strong sense of belonging with the 'blacks' strengthen her rage and incompatibility towards the whites or any other racial or cultural groups. On the contrary, her physique prevents her from identifying herself with the blacks, eventually, her psyche refrains her from relating herself to the whites as well. It manifested itself into a state of "identity disregard" according to which an individual is seen continuously "ignoring" or "neglecting" any sense of identity with others (Sen, 20).

Gloria Naylor, through her male characters like Fuller and Woods, tries to portray the ever-persisting intense psychological turbulences of what she calls it, to be a "scarred psychology" (Ashford, 86). These characters of colour in Naylor's The Women of Brewster Place seems to be deeply affected by the prevailing adverse notions of Colonialism and Eurocentrism. The notions, for ages, have developed a negative impact on the minds of a black, colonizing their psychology and accordingly streamlining their thoughts. Thus the thought of a man of colour regarding himself and his physical appearance is always shaped on negative grounds, generating a kind of shame for himself and his entire race. This is the result of the deep-rooted psychological upheaval taking place among the blacks as a result of racism.

Apart from the "scarred psychology" of Kiswana, this implicit form of long-condensed and genetically-transmitted psychological abuse is seen in the daily conversations and dialogues of these male characters like Butch Fuller and also in the prayers of Reverend Woods. For instance, in a conversation between Mattie Michael and Butch Fuller (in the 1st section of the novel entitled 'Mattie Michael'), while they were walking under the scorching sun of April and Fuller was trying to protect his skin from getting dark in the sun, he asserts, "Too much sun on the main road,[...] And since black means poor in these parts–Lord knows, I couldn't stand to get no poorer" (12). A similar outcome of the deep-seated psychological violence is cited in the speech of Reverend Woods when he, while in the process of preaching delivers these lines, "Yes, Lord–grind out the unheated tenements! Merciful Jesus– shove aside the low-paying boss man. Perfect Father fill me, fill me till there's no room, no room for nothing else, not even that great big world out there that exacts such a strange penalty for my being born black" (65).

This way, Naylor extends the Euro-centric notions of blackness through the dialogues and thoughts of her characters that are so much burdened with a load of such notions in the form of psychological violence that they are bound to reflect through their daily conversations and psychologies. Here violence resulting from racism in the form of psychological destruction is seen as a driving force for the generation of dialogues in the novel.

The "Unstrung Puppet": Sexual Violation and Racism

In the novel, the problem of multiculturalism is subtly dealt with a biangular discourse in the section entitled "The Two". While the first angle is grounded in the context of the differences in skin colour of 'the two, the second is fueled by the uncanny sexuality shared between 'the two women. Here, "The Two", stands both as a suitable title for a particular section in the novel as well as for the lesbian couple– Lorraine and Theresa. Naylor is very particular in her description of the external features of these two characters. She describes Lorraine as "the lighter, skinny one" who was "readily accepted" (129) by the women of Brewster Place. Theresa on the other hand is described as "the short dark one––too pretty, and too much behind", for whom "breaths were held a little longer" (129). The phrases apparently tend to be describing the physical attributes of the two ladies. Though at a deeper level, it is a more racist approach abusing the doctrine of multiculturalism. The bodies of these women, therefore become a reflection of one's own (racist) perception, the stereotypes governing human existence, as it is truly said that, "women's bodies [the black women in particular], in patriarchal societies, are fashioned into conventional notions of femininity, and if the body resists the disciplining process, "subtle coercion" is exercised" (Ghosh et al., 2017, 219).

Lorrain's "lighter" skin colour and "skinny" body type associate her more to a white occidental woman than to a black woman of colour. On the other hand, there's a "dark" complexion and "short" body type with "too much behind" associates her with a woman of colour, thereby projecting her as the typical oriental woman of the East. A more realist approach of the portrayal reflected racism when the author describes Theresa pertaining to the stereotypical norms of a black female body objectifying and presenting it as something that the black feminist critics like Hooks term to be "transgressive", "promiscuous" or "sexually deviant" (Hooks, 1982; Young, 2007), when Naylor further writes, "And she insisted on wearing those thin Qiana dresses that the summer breeze moulded against the maddening rhythm of the twenty pounds of rounded flesh that swung steadily down the street" (129-130).

Apart from their opposing physical appearance both Lorraine and Theresa participate equally in the bond of homosexuality that exists between the two. Lorraine, because of her skin colour and body type that resembles the occidental woman is viewed as an 'other's-other' in the conservative black society of Brewster Place. In relation to the multicultural context, Lorraine is viewed under two lights, one as an 'occidental' and the other as a 'lesbian', where both sets her culturally out of the mainstream. Even though Theresa's black body is stereotypically viewed as something that Hooks calls "expendable" with its "accessibility" and "availability" (Young, 2007, 13) the trauma of rape befalls solely upon the shoulders of Lorraine, assuming her to be the most suitable victim. By violating Lorrain's "tall" and "yellow" body, C. C. Baker and his friends consider that they have culturally overpowered the "others". This ironic ideology of cultural overpowering is reflected through the dialogues of Baker when he persistently abuses Lorraine while raping her, "I am gonna show you somethin' I bet you have never seen before." C.C. Baker takes the back of her head, presses it into the crotch of his jeans, and jerkily rubs it back and forth while his friends laugh, "Yeah, now don't that feel good? See, that's what you need. But after we get through you, you are never gonna wanna kiss no more pussy" (TWBP, 1983, 170).

Such abusive lingual addressing reflects a faulty cultural overpowering of patriarchy over heterosexuality (lesbianism) where the former tries to restore his lost hegemony over the latter through sexual violence. This idea of violence against gay and lesbians is dealt with in one of the sections (entitled 'Violence against Gay and Lesbian People') in Beckett and Macey's essay Race, Gender and Sexuality: The Oppression of Multiculturalism". According to this analysis, the society and its people (in particular those adhering to the Qu'ran and the Bible) "see it as their duty to physically harm people who are not heterosexual" (2001, p. 313). While regarding the physical (ie., the racial and colour) context, the rape of Lorraine reminds us of the episode of the rape of Lynne in Alice Walker's Meridian.

Like the rape of Lynne, Lorrain's rape too, can be read as a black man's fallacious act for his "need to liberate himself from white oppression by taking revenge upon white women" (Lauretqtd. in Tanritanir and Aydemir, 2012). The other female characters in the novel, like Ben's daughter Etta, and Mattie too, endure sexual violations in the garb of either slavery or marriage or maybe through the expression of momentary love. While Ben's daughter embraces sexual harassment by a white master as a compromise at the hands of her poverty, Etta is used for physical gratification by Woods suggesting false intentions of marriage. Also, Mattie is made to offer her virginity to Butch just to fetch his thirst that always lusted for her "full round breasts" (17) and "high round behind" (9).

In all the cases of rape and sexual assault of these women of Brewster Place, the root cause of violence is seen to be arrested in the issue of multiculturalism that attacks the harmonious cultural hybridity of a society nurturing racism and intolerance. While Lorraine's rape was a result of racial intolerance, the sexual use of Ben's daughter, Etta and Mattie depict the racial segregation of black women projecting them as what Hooks calls the most "undesirable" yet the most "accessible" beings as per the established Euro-centric norms (Hooks, 1982). Black men tend to rape their own women in their own frustrations as a result of their "scarred psychologies" that generates from these cultural differences. While dealing with the atrocities inflicted on the black women, the writer intends to "touch(es) upon the larger black feminine sensibilities. She narrates the lives of these women with a purpose– to legitimize their female self, its history and culture. In the process of unravelling the hidden histories of the characters, she invents a new poetics" (Sonal and Singh,

2017, 209).

CONCLUSION

According to critics like Markus, Plaut, Wolsko et al., the notion of multiculturalism was established to stress the importance of cultural diversities, the recognition of diverse ethnic, racial and cultural groups and the explicit valuing of this diversity in the mainstream settings. This traditional ideology, though many times seemed to fail in achieving its proposed goals. According to Plaut's unfavourable concept of multiculturalism, it is defined as something that stands in contrast to the so assumed concept of 'colour-blindness' that overlooks any existing differentiation in terms of one's skin colour. Multiculturalism thus celebrates differences, intolerance and violence. A report on multiculturalism under the study of the American Nationalist Party, read by the heading, 'Multiculturalism, Racism, Violence and Balkanization', attacks its ideology of racial differences claiming multiculturalism to have been at its strongest when racism is at its best. It also proclaims that multiculturalism is the highest form of racism.

Writers have taken this issue as a nexus for their discussion to portray one's historical, social and personal predicaments. In the case of some of the black female writers and black women in general, it goes "indisputable that their own victimization has led these women towards social activism" (Das and Singh, 2016, 219). Though multiculturalism projects its diverse discourses both good and bad, Gloria Naylor still finds herself and her entire race struggling under the scars of racism and slavery (Carabi, 1991). Her novel The Women of Brewster Place thus projects the problem of multiculturalism that degrades the larger human race necessarily leading to violence, thereby portraying violence as an embedded discourse of Multiculturalism.

Works Cited

Ashford, Tomeiko R. (2005). "Gloria Naylor on Black Spirituality: An Interview".

MELUS, 30(4),7387.Retrieved from http://www.jstor.org/stable/30029635

Beckett, Clare. and MarieMacey (2001)."Race, Gender and Sexuality: The Oppression of Multiculturalism". Women's Studies International Forum 24(3/4), 309319.

Carabi, Angels. (1991). "Interview with Gloria Naylor."Revista de Estudios Norte americanos.n., 23-35.

Das, Ankita. and Rajni Singh (2016)."Empowering Lives: The Journey of Jaycee Dugard, Elizabeth Smart, and Mukhtar Mai" .Journal of Dharma 41(1), 201-220

Ghosh, Soumya M. and Rajni Singh. (2017). "Violated Bodies and the Reclamation of Female UshaGanguli's Ham Mukhtārā and Maya Krishna Rao's Walk".Archiv Orientalni 85,219-252.

Hooks, Bell (1982). Ain't I A Woman: Black Woman and Feminism. Pluto Press: London.

Naylor, Gloria. (1983). The women of Brewster Place. U.S.A: Penguin books. Subjectivity in

Niru Sharan, Violence Against Women and the Laws in India, IMPACT: International Journal of Research in Humanities, Arts and Literature (IMPACT: IJRHAL), Volume 5, Issue 7, July 2017, pp. 197-202

Sen, Amartya. (2007). Identity and Violence: The Illusion of Destiny. U.S.A: Penguin Books.

Sonal, Smrity.and Rajni Singh (2017)."Black Female Bodies and Resistance in

Gayl Jones' Corregidora and Eva's Man".Rupkatha: Journal on Interdisciplinary Studies in Humanities9(2),203-211.Retrieved from https://dx.doi.org/10.21659/rupkatha.v9n2.21

Tanritanir, Bulent C.and Y. Aydemir (2012). "The Suffers of Black Women in

Alice Walker's Color Purple and Meridian and Toni Morrison's Novels Beloved and The Novels the Bluest Eye".The Journal of International Social Research 5(23).437-444.

Rajesh Kumar MD, Domestic Violence Against Women in Indian Context:

Causes and Impact on Family, IMPACT: International Journal of Research in Applied, Natural and Social Sciences (IMPACT: IJRANSS), Volume 5, Issue 8, August 2017, p. 27-34

Young, Tiffany Ann (2007). Rape in Contemporary American Literature: Writing

Women As Florida State University)Electronic Theses, Treaties and Dissertations. Paper 868.

Sonal, Smrity and Singh, Rajni, Violence, an Embedded Discourse of Multiculturalism in Gloria

Naylor's The Women of Brewster Place (February 3, 2018). IMPACT: International Journal of Research in Humanities, Arts and Literature, Vol. 6, Issue 2, February 2018, 257-262 , Available at SSRN: https://ssrn.com/abstract=3133494

SHARING SIMILARITIES, CELEBRATING DIFFERENCES: A SEARCH FOR THE SELF IN BABY KAMBLE'S THE PRISONS WE BROKE AND LAKSHMIBAI TILAK'S I FOLLOW AFTER

Mrs. Deepti Mujumdar

Department Head of English

Chikitsak Samuha's Patkar-Varde College, Mumbai.

ABSTRACT

All of us know and understand that there exists an intimate and vital connection between literature and life and that literature is an expression of individual and social life and thought through language. Good literature is always appreciated for the length and breadth of life it paints, the ways in which it grasps and reflects the truths of life that emerge triumphant out of the ruins of the past, and the way it emancipates the human mind from its limitations. Since autobiography as a genre explores the nexus of life, language and literature in an interesting manner, this paper focuses on the search for the self in two autobiographies by women writers – one a Dalit woman and the other an upper-caste brahmin woman.

Keywords: autobiography, women and self.

• • •

"Sharing Similarities, Celebrating Differences" - A Search for the Self in Baby Kamble's The Prisons We Broke and

Lakshmibai Tilak's I follow After

This paper is divided into four sections – the first section discusses Autobiography as a genre, the second focuses on Autobiography as a chosen medium of expression by women writers, the third section introduces the two texts selected and the last section compares and contrasts the texts to bring out the intended meaning of the title of the paper, "Sharing Similarities, Celebrating Differences". Though not very easy to define, autobiography in the broader sense of the word is used almost synonymously with "life writing" and denotes all modes and genres of telling one's own life. More specifically, autobiography as a literary genre signifies a retrospective narrative that undertakes to tell the author's own life, or a substantial part of it, seeking, to a certain extent, to reconstruct his/her personal development within a given historical, social and cultural framework.

The emergence of autobiography as a literary genre and critical term coincides with what has frequently been called the emergence of the modern subject around 1800. Since then, it has evolved as a genre of non-fictional, yet 'constructed' auto diegetic (narrator who is also the protagonist) narration wherein a self-reflective subject enquires into his/her identity and its developmental trajectory. While autobiography on the one hand claims to be non-fictional (factual) in that it proposes to tell the story of a 'real' person, it is inevitably constructive, or imaginative, in nature and as a form of textual 'self-fashioning' ultimately resists a clear distinction from its fictional relatives (autofiction, autobiographical novel), leaving the generic borderlines blurred.

Autobiography constructs an individual life course as a coherent, meaningful whole. Even if autobiography's aspect of re-living experience, of rendering incidents as they were experienced at the time, is considered, the superior 'interpreting' position of the narrative present remains paramount, turning past events into a meaningful plot, making sense of contingency. The field of life writing as narratives of self—or of various forms of self—has now become significantly broader, transcending the classic model of autobiographical identity qua coherent retrospective narrative. Yet whatever its theoretical remodelling and practical rewritings, even if frequently subverted in practice, maybe, the close nexus between narrative, self/identity, and the genre/practice of autobiography continues to be considered paramount. The underlying assumption concerning autobiography is that of a close, even inextricable connection between narrative and identity, with autobiography the prime generic site of enactment.

A lot of notions about autobiography as a narrative genre have been challenged with the emergence of new theories and perspectives – like gender studies and the postcolonial and subaltern theories. If gender studies exposed autobiography's individualist self as a phenomenon of male self-fashioning, a postcolonial theory further challenged its universal validity. While autobiography was long considered an exclusively Western genre, postcolonial approaches to autobiography/ life writing have significantly expanded the corpus of autobiographical writings and provided a perspective that is critical of both the eurocentrism of autobiography genre theory and the concepts of selfhood in operation (Lionett, 1991).

In this context, too, the question has arisen as to how autobiography is possible for those who have no voice of their own, who cannot speak for themselves (whom Spivak calls the 'subaltern'). Such 'Writing ordinary lives', usually aiming at collective identities, poses specific problems: sociological, ethical and even aesthetic (Pandian 2008). Whatever the markers of difference and semantic foci explored, the notion of autobiography has shifted from literary genre to a broad range of cultural practices that draw on and incorporate a multitude of textual modes and genres. By 2001, Smith and Watson (eds. 2001) were able to list fifty-two "Genres of Life Narrative" by combining formal and semantic features. Among them are narratives of migration, immigration or exile, narratives engaging with ethnic identity and community, prison narratives, illness, trauma and coming-out narratives as much as celebrity memoirs, graphic life writing and forms of Internet self-presentation. These multiple forms and practices produce, or allow critics to freshly address, new 'subject formations' within specific historical and cultural localities.

In Writing a Woman's Life, Carolyn G. Heilburn says that a woman's life can be described in four ways: "... the women herself may tell it, in what she chooses to call an autobiography; she may tell it in what she chooses to call fiction; a biographer, woman or man, may write a biography, or the woman may write her own life in advance of living it, unconsciously and without realising or naming the process". A woman's autobiography generally deals with the various relationships like those with her parents, siblings and with her spouse, children and other women of her family. Her identity is established only based on these relationships. A man's autobiography is mainly concerned with his success story, achievements, and the world of work. He rarely focuses on his familial relationships.

Although each author may have significant, sometimes dazzling accomplishments to her credit, the theme of accomplishment rarely dominates the narrative.... Indeed to a striking degree, they fail directly to emphasize their own importance, though writing in a genre which implies self-assertion and self-display.

George Henry Lewes says that a woman's literature 'promises a woman's view of life, woman's experience: in other words, a new element'. But he further adds, "Masculine mind is characterized by the predominance of intellect and the feminine by the predominance of emotions... Woman, by her greater affectionateness, her greater range and depth of emotional experience, is well fitted to give expression to the emotional facts of life" (9). But is that all that a woman autobiography writer has to offer? Fortunately, no. When a woman chooses to write an autobiography, she is making a conscious choice. An autobiography enables women to correct the histories of their lives, enables them to introspect, think deeply about their lives and develop a positive self-identity. Writing an autobiography becomes a therapeutic process. It becomes a weapon of self-assertion, a political act, helpful in achieving a sense of identity and mobilizing resistance against different forms of oppression. It provides a rounded and complete picture of the Self, located in a community with which it is symbiotically linked and in the process the writer also becomes a Social Historian.

The first text being reviewed is an autobiography by Lakshmibai Tilak, published in the 1930s in Marathi and translated later in English by E. Josephine Inkster. In Marathi, the work is titled Smriti Chitre which can be loosely translated as 'Glimpses of my Memory' or 'As I remember. However, the title of the translated work I

Follow After has resulted in a general interpretation that the narrative is a story of a self-effacing woman, following the path led by her husband, without questioning. Reading against the grain, the narrative tells the story of the triumph of an independent woman who wants to lead a life on her own terms. beneath the superficial chatty and humorous narrative, there is a narrative of pain and sufferings, there is a story of resistance to the social norms that govern life and a transformation to a newer and more satisfying world views, which is a personal choice quite contrary to the prevalent social norms.

Lakshmi begins her narrative with the description of her stifled childhood experiences under the persecution of her eccentric father. Her childhood description, if read carefully can be seen as the portrayal of pain and sufferings of her mother, her grandmother and of other children of the household but Lakshmi's chatty and racy tone gives it a different hue and the pain gets encrusted in humour. At the same time, she gives a detailed account of her mother's generous, amiable and rational disposition that was the source of solace for all.

I Follow After is characterised by the elaboration of every trifle issue of the banal life. It seems such elaboration of trivial helped her to give the description of many obnoxious realities quite naturally, which would otherwise be impossible to talk about if she had relied on precise and to the point depiction, without causing outrage. Lakshmibai Tilak belongs to a nineteenth-century orthodox society of Maharashtra, where religion was a sacrosanct affair and anyone challenging it was punished by ostracism from society. In such a milieu it was really a momentous task for a person, especially a woman from a peculiar Brahmanical background to cross the religion and caste boundaries and to adopt Christianity. Lakshmi's husband Narayan Waman Tilak, a famous poet of his time opted for Christianity and his conversion

Lakshmibai Tilak's autobiography manages to draw a comprehensive portrait of the husband. Rev.Tilak, as the book portrays him, is a multifaceted personality- a poet who can write poems in the act of speaking, an actor whose performance in a play can move the audience to tears, an eloquent orator who wins a number of prizes in elocution competitions, a great teacher whose teaching can turn even urchins into poets. Apart from that, he is also a man of vanity who seems to value respect and honour a lot and to fear that everyone is out to insult him, a man with a sense of humour, absent-minded, irascible, impractical, courageous, unconventional, spiritual, a loving but whimsical husband. Though she praises her husband at every stage and gives all credit to him for guiding her in her life, she does not hesitate to comment on his whimsical nature and criticize his behaviour. Though her husband wants her to convert to Christianity as he does, Lakshmi resists and is able to hold her fort against his wishes. His conversion creates a lot of clamour in Lakshmi's life. She faces all these with her indomitable spirit and logical disposition. Commenting about her restorative capacity, she writes, "Many and many a time I had been on the point of forsaking this earthly body, but I had never actually done it, and I believe it was never possible. It was characteristic of me to grope on through the darkness of despair, but still to keep to the road. It was not me to lie down and die halfway. In short, I rebounded like a rubber ball" (40).

Her choice of converting to Christianity is lighted by her understanding and consciousness. By adopting Christianity she tries to free herself from all bondages of caste and religion. Her conversion is the proof of her tenacity, independence of mind and the inherent spirit of rebellion, which according to Susie Tharu and K. Lalitha, "she had inherited from her grandfather, Vasudev Bhagwat Jogelkar, who was hanged in the aftermath of 1857 Sepoy Rebellion." (Tharu and Lalitha, 309)

The autobiography can be seen as a tale of twofold transformation of a woman – one from a simple and docile housewife to a self-conscious and self-sufficient woman leading and managing her life on her own accord. The other transformation is in terms of her adoption of the broad world view of Christianity leaving the narrow and superstitious outlook of Hinduism, as experienced by her in her interaction with her family and society of that time. The main intent of her writing seems to enumerate both physical and mental struggles such transformations involved and also to subtly document her triumphant emergence, overcoming all these. Her conversion to Christianity widens her perspective and provides her insight into the empathetic stance of Christianity towards women. Such insights helped her in retrospective analysis through the lens of Christianity, the sufferings of her mother, her mother- in –law and also her own at the hands of the patriarchs of the household, and through her narrative, she has given voice to all these silent sufferings.

The second text being discussed is by a Dalit woman writer Babytai Kamble and its title is The Prisons We Broke. Originally written in Marathi and published in 1986 as Jeena Amucha , it was translated by Dr. Maya Pandit and published in English in 2008. Her words, firmly rooted in the Ambedkarite ideology, have continued to inspire Dalit activists to this day, urging them to look beyond the individual to the community in the struggle for freedom and equality. Her autobiography is path-breaking for being the first critique of twofold patriarchy – an experience of Dalit women's lives recognizing their dual oppression by caste and gender.

Like an auto-ethnographer, Baby gives a detailed description of the houses, the locality of the houses in the village: the Maharwada, the restrictions faced by Mahars in the other parts of the village or even in their area in the presence of a higher caste man. She narrates all this not just from the experience of being a Mahar, but a Mahar woman.

She identifies the notions of double consciousness within the Mahar women. Although 'Hindu philosophy had discarded us as dirt and thrown us into their garbage pits, on the outskirts of the village' yet Mahar women desperately tried to preserve whatever bits of Hindu culture they could imitate so that they would be able to live like the upper caste, enjoy wealth like their wives and practice their rituals. She is aware that these rituals marked their difference from the upper caste and they were denied to them to keep them suppressed. At the same time, the Mahar women imitated the Hindu rituals as 'an outlet for their oppressed souls'.

Her narration is from the various angles of the self's experience, shared experience from women of her community and her own observations. This covers in it the temporal span of her childhood and adult life which also brilliantly captures the experience of her community and the women of her community at the height of Dr Ambedkar's revolutionary leadership and beyond. There is in her story a history of a great leader and the Dalit movement under his able and revered leadership, and later a lament for the way the movement had lost its aim in the political mayhem and personal agendas of the people of the community itself, but there is hope too for the re-emergence of the movement of pride and dignity.

Babytai is outspoken and does not dilute her narration in the self-glorification of the community. Rather she is critical of the community, its behaviour towards its women, towards its way of life. While she tells the story of her father who was educated and ready to sweat it out in his work as a contractor for buildings, she also brings out the helping nature of his which at times would leave the family with nothing to eat. She portrays the anguish of the women against the hardships and poverty in the sharp remarks of her mother for her father who would never save (he would always say that one does not need more than a bellyful). The helpless requests of the mothers of the poorer families (who would ask their husbands to get some cactus flowers to cook) at the same time shows the terrible side of the same women as mothers-in-law.

Babytai gives us a dark picture of the situation of a Mahar girl—married at a young age; devoid of education to stand for self; beaten and bruised by in-laws and husband; working long hours; getting whatever is left over after families consumption, and undergoing regular pregnancies where she has no choice. All this leaves her at the bottom of the ladder of development. Her movement curtailed and under surveillance very much the same as that of women from the upper caste, her sexuality controlled by her family and relatives through taunts and thrashings, her position as the last in the family from basic consumption to decision making, the Mahar women is under the dual burden of her caste and her sexuality.

Baby breaks the myth of a democratic Dalit family. She brings out the inhumane acts of the chopping off of the nose of women by the husband and his family; the regular burden of torture and taunts. She remarks that in the days prior to the 1940s that at least one woman in a hundred would have her nose chopped off by the husband under the provocation of his mother or father. The overall condition of women is pitiable not just because of the troubles they have with the other castes but also because of an existing disrespect for women at large. Women have to bear the burden of purity; they could be questioned if they do not veil themselves properly, called a 'slut' by the men and women for any shortcoming (the connotation of the word 'slut' itself is derogatory to women only; there is no mention of an equivalent term for the male). It has been an enigma how a community which is obsessed with the worship of the Goddess and celebrates the possession of the bodies of their women by Goddesses can butcher the same body as filthy and polluted.

In Baby's autobiography, there is a tension between tradition and modernity to which the Mahars respond with the determination to achieve modernity. This modernity is embodied by Ambedkar and is epitomised by him. Again there are traditional structures within the community such as the chawdi (30) which is very much a modern concept of public space available for debates and deliberation. The change in the space of action, dialogue and doing: here the schoolboys plan their temple entry; here the Mahar wada[31] celebrate their first Ambedkar's birth anniversary; here, Baby and her husband start the first shop of their wada as a protest against the shopkeepers of the village who practised untouchability. It is also the place of traditional get-togethers and celebrations.

The work mostly revolves around the day-to-day lives of the Mahar community; the perpetual shortage of food, battered, stitched together pieces of rags as dresses, the snot-nosed and dirty children, the trials and methods of bringing home food from collections of leftovers; in exchange of labour, collection of dead animals during epidemics, to poisoning someone's cattle in the most difficult situation. The autobiography speaks of the lives of the Mahar people, their traditions, celebrations, their Gods and Goddesses. A large part of the work consists of retelling myths and stories around evil forces, superstitions and the belief of the people in forces that write their destiny, difficult processes of treatment in case of ill health. According to Baby Kamble, Mahars opt for these beliefs, superstitions and treatments in the face of want and needs. They have no money or means for alternatives.

Baby never mentions her own life events—marriage, the birth of children—except for her own birth. However, she mentions her enrolment in school; her experience in a new school with caste-Hindu girls; the opening of their shop in the Maharwada—the first one. She writes of her decision to be equally involved in the shop; her decision to write about her experiences; the decision to send her children to school; their success in the academic and professional world; her involvement and service for the community in terms of running a government-supported orphanage for the backward caste. These are significant events in her life.

Baby Kamble breaks the boundary of given notions of womanhood and creates a self that dares to challenge the given. In her choice of significant life events, she mentions those events which she has imbibed as important from her close engagement with Ambedkar's thoughts. As she affirms, 'I made a firm resolve, at a young age to lead my life according the path sketched by Dr. Babasaheb Ambedkar, the light of my life. His principles have exercised a strong influence on me.' It was his principles of education, economic independence and political participation of Dalits and especially Dalit women, that worked as her framework for her life and hence life events. Baby Kamble narrates her and her community's shared experience of breaking prohibitions, internalised and imposed—' the prisons'—that excluded them. It is the prisons of hunger, illiteracy, untouchability, patriarchy, economic dependency, superstition, disease and social disability related to caste and gender that they broke. It is through the breaking of these prisons that the Dalit, including the Dalit women, assert their selfhood. Thus, both Lakshmibai Tilak and Babytai Kamble become social historians, giving the readers glimpses of the society and the milieu they belonged to – one does it subtly and almost unconsciously, while the other makes it her main intention of writing.

We see both Lakshmibai and Babytai resisting the norms of the society, at times even at the cost of pain and suffering at the hands of their immediate families. It is their strong, indomitable spirit that keeps them going. Both the autobiographies speak of conversion. People have criticised Lakshmibai's decision to convert to Christianity as being solely influenced by her husband. But what they fail to see is how she resisted her husband's attempt to convert her and prefers a life of separation from him, while enduring constant humiliation and pain from her family. It is only when she herself is convinced of the worldview upheld by Christianity does she decide to convert and this surprises even her husband. Thus, it is a very conscious and rational reason as is Baby Kamble's decision to convert to Buddhism based on her understanding of Ambedkarite ideology.

Lakshmibai's son wanted to write his father's biography and hence needed his mother to describe his father as she remembered her. So Lakshmibai starts writing about her husband, but the act soon becomes a way for her to talk about her life as well. Again, people have criticised her by saying that if she were to write about her life exclusively still she wouldn't have been able to write any differently for she had merged her identity with her husband. Sadly, these people only read superficially and are largely misled by the title I Follow After. Lakshmibai's autobiography, though paints a positive image of her husband, yet it largely talks of her independent decision making, her social work and her life after his death as well. Staying within the framework of her milieu, Lakshmibai chooses a language with humorous undertones and speaks what is there on her mind. Babytai, though very outspoken in her narrative, has to hide her writings from her husband because her husband is well. 'just like any other husband!'

Kamble's autobiography shows a greater awareness of the socio-political movements of her age than Tilak's and projects a self that is intrinsically linked with the community. Lakshmibai Tilak's work is more personal and projects a self that desires to change and does change due to her willingness and assertion. Both the works are remarkable in their projection of a strong self, and it will be wrong trying to judge who does a better job while forgetting the different social milieu these two women came from. Both are imperfect and boldly acknowledge this fact whiling commenting on the imperfections of others. But they inspire in their own unique way. Hence, we need to celebrate their differences and appreciate the lessons they give.

Works Cited

Bamberg, Michael (2011). "Who am I? Narration and its contribution to self and identity." Theory & Psychology 21.1, 3–24.

"The Autobiographical Process." R. Folkenflik (ed.). The Culture of Autobiography: Constructions of Self-Representations. Stanford: Stanford UP, 28–56.Burke, Peter (2011).

"Rethinking narrative identity." M. Klepper & C. Holler (eds.). Rethinking Narrative Identity. Persona and Perspective. Amsterdam: John Benjamins, 1–31.Kohli, Martin (1981).

On Autobiography. Minneapolis: U of Minnesota P.Lionett, Françoise (1991).

Sharmila Rege, Writing Caste/Writing Gender: Dalit Women's Testimonies, New Delhi: Zubaan, 2006.

S Punalekar, 'The sociology of Dalit autobiography', in Social Transformation in India: Essays in Honour of Professor I.P. Desai, edited by. G. Shah, Jaipur: Rawat Publishers, 1993, pp. 371–96.

Conditions and Limits of Autobiography, Autobiography: Essays Theoretical and critical Ed. James Olney, Princeton university press, 1980.

Susie Tharu and K. Lalita, eds., Women Writing in India: 600 B.C to the Present. Volume 1: 600 B.C to the Early Twentieth Century. New York: Feminist Press, 1991. Volume 2: The Twentieth Century. Feminist Press, 1993.

Bio-Note

Mrs. Deepti Mujumdar is currently the Head of the Department of English at Chikitsak Samuha's Patkar-Varde College (Autonomous), Mumbai. She has teaching experience of 20 years at UG and 12 years at the PG level. She has published 17 research articles in various Peer-reviewed National and International journals and has co-authored a book titled "An anthology of Indian Poetry". Her core area of research is feminism and other areas of specialisation are post-colonialism and gender studies. Mrs.

Deepti Mujumdar is a blogger and is currently focusing on "Revisiting Indian Mythology", wherein she takes a look at the stories through a feminist lens. These blogs have been appreciated internationally, with over 5000 views in four months. She is also a winner of four National Awards for education and social work.